1001 PROMPTS FOR UNLOCKING GENERATIVE AI IN LOCAL GOVERNMENT

Micah Gaudet

Civic.AI

Visit www.CivicInnovation.ai for the first-ever course focused on ChatGPT and Generative AI in the public sector.

CONTENTS

PREFACE

Recent advances in artificial intelligence have led to the development of large language models (LLMs) that can understand context and generate human-like text. ChatGPT, built on the foundation of LLMs, offers new potential to serve as interactive decision support systems that can aid in analysis, provide recommendations, and enhance knowledge for users. However, effectively utilizing these tools requires an understanding of how they work, their limitations, and the importance of proper prompt engineering. This paper provides an overview of LLMs, their capabilities as decision support systems, prompt engineering techniques, and key considerations for their effective use.

LLMs like ChatGPT are trained on massive text datasets, allowing them to learn nuanced patterns of language and grammar. This training enables LLMs to interpret the context of provided prompts and generate relevant and coherent responses. When given a user input, LLMs preprocess and encode the text into contextual representations that a decoder then uses to produce output text that responds appropriately to the prompt.

LLMs can thus simulate conversational dialogues, answer questions on a wide range of topics, and generate content when given the proper prompts. However, they also have limitations, including potential inaccuracies, biases extracted from training data, and difficulty with highly ambiguous or unstructured prompts. Utilizing LLMs effectively requires understanding their capabilities and limitations.

LLMs possess several key attributes that make them well-suited for decision support functions. They can integrate data from various sources, analyze text and interpret questions, provide interactive dialogue for clarification, offer evidence-based suggestions, and tailor responses to specific needs. As such, they can augment human decision-making by providing fast access to knowledge, summarizations of lengthy reports, and informed recommendations based on user parameters.

However, some care should be taken in relying solely on LLM recommendations for high-stakes decisions. Fact checking and validating with domain experts is advisable. LLMs may struggle with novel situations outside their training, and they ultimately only provide options not final decisions. Integrating LLMs as part of a robust process can enhance decision quality but not replace human judgment.

To function effectively as decision support tools, LLMs need to be guided with well-designed prompts. Prompts serve as instructions that shape how models respond, so crafting clear, specific prompts is key. Effective prompts provide necessary context, clear goals and parameters, optimal length and tone specifications, and examples to elicit the desired output.

Templates can help structure sound prompts, and iteration based on initial outputs is often needed to refine prompts for improved results. Precision in prompt engineering is required to translate needs into interactions that generate high-quality LLM responses. This process takes experimentation but allows users to unlock LLMs' potential.

LLMs present new opportunities to enhance decision-making through their ability to process information, provide interactive dialogue, and offer data-driven recommendations. However, prompt engineering is essential to guide these tools effectively. Carefully optimizing prompts can allow public agencies to leverage LLMs while mitigating risks and limitations. With appropriate design and diligent monitoring, integrating LLMs as part of robust governance processes holds much promise for improving knowledge and analysis to tackle complex public challenges.

Local governments across the United States stand at the threshold of a technological renaissance. With the advent of generative AI—embodied by chatbots like ChatGPT, Claude, and Bard—municipalities are embracing tools that promise not only to streamline administration but also to revolutionize citizen engagement.

My journey into the realm of AI began rather modestly. It was a YouTube video on ChatGPT that first piqued my interest. Initially a source of bedtime stories for my child and a generator of light-hearted dad jokes, it wasn't long before the professional applications of this technology became apparent.

While generative AI's potential is vast, its implementation is fraught with challenges unique to the public sector. Whether it's the diverse community needs from San Jose to Waco or the myriad of state-specific laws, one-size-fits-all solutions are nonstarters. Legal constraints and the specter of AI bias further complicate the landscape, necessitating a tailored approach for each jurisdiction.

A casual conversation with a friend and fellow City Manager evolved into a full-fledged webinar, attracting hundreds of viewers and igniting a broader conversation on AI's role in local governance. This book is an extension of that dialogue. That has since led to the creation of the first course on Generative AI specifically designed for the public sector (available at www.civicinnovaiton.ai). This book is simply a next step in my work. It aims to provide local governments with actionable prompts to integrate AI thoughtfully and responsibly into their daily operations.

Adopting AI is not merely a question of technological readiness but also of strategic clarity. As municipalities, we need to shift our focus from job retention to performance optimization. Generative AI should be seen not as a threat but as an enabler—a tool that amplifies human capabilities, allowing skilled professionals to focus on value-added activities that enhance public services and build community trust.

This book serves as a guide for those at the helm of this transformative shift. Comprising 1001 prompts, it offers actionable insights for various functional areas within local governance. From public safety and community development to economic planning and beyond, these prompts are designed to inspire, provoke thought, and serve as a starting point for meaningful action.

The age of AI in local government is upon us. Let's embrace it with the responsibility, accountability, and vision it demands.

Thank you for joining me on this journey.

Micah Gaudet

Deputy City Manager and Advocate for AI in Local Government

1001 Prompts for Unlocking Generative AI in Local Government

By Micah Gaudet

HUMAN RESOURCES

1. I am the Human Resources director for the city of ____. I want to create a new employee orientation checklist. please create the checklist

2. I am a City Manager and I need to create a policy on acceptable use of work email for city employees. Please help me draft the policy.

3. You are a City Manager in ____. Write a memo to the Human Resources Director. The Memo should provide directions to move forward with the recruitment of an Assistant City Manager using the services of ____ recruitment firm. The HR director should review and propose updates to the job description. The changes should be sent to the City Manager for final approval. HR Director should then work with the City's communications team and ___ firm to create a visually appealing and engaging job ad, and brochure that highlights the benefits of working in Ennis as well as the future challenges facing the city.

4. You are a Human Resources Director for the city of ____. Your job is to write a job description for a Budget Analyst. We want this position to prioritize accountability and fiscal responsibility.

5. Create a session handout for a training on ____

6. [upload public sector workforce data from the US Census Bureau] Compare the number of full-time, part-time, and full-time equivalent employees in each government function for the state of Alaska. Recommend and create 2 visualizations to help me analyze this info.

7. You are a City Manager in Oak Harbor, WA. Write a memo to the Human Resources Director. The Memo should provide directions to move forward with the recruitment of an Assistant City Manager using the services of Strategic Government Resources. The HR director should review and propose updates to the job description. The changes should be sent to the City Manager for final approval. The HR Director should then work with the City's communications team and SGR to create a visually appealing and engaging job ad, and brochure that highlights the benefits of working in Ennis as well as the future challenges facing the city.

8. Propose a training program for customer service improvement for parks and recreation staff in the city of ___.

9. I am an HR analyst for the city of ___. Suggest an employee wellness program.

10. I am an HR analyst for ___ county, describe how to update sexual harassment prevention training.

11. I am the Director of Administration for the County of ___. How can we measure and improve employee performance?

12. I am the Deputy County Manager for ___. What are some cost-effective ways to increase employee engagement?

13. Incorporating a culture of safety within public works is crucial. How can we develop and sustain a safety-focused environment that prioritizes the well-being of our employees?

14. Boosting worker morale and job satisfaction is essential for a motivated workforce. What innovative strategies or initiatives can be implemented to enhance the overall job experience for our employees?

15. You're the Employee Benefits Optimization Specialist in Willowbrook Valley. Discuss strategies to optimize the employee benefits package within budget constraints.

16. How can we improve employee retention while managing costs?

17. How can we improve the employee onboarding process?

18. Describe a strategy for reducing employee turnover rates.

19. I am working on innovative methods for employee recognition and rewards in Norman, Oklahoma. Can you suggest creative approaches for recognizing and rewarding employees?

20. I am working on a plan for increasing employee engagement in St. Cloud, Minnesota. Can you propose effective steps to boost employee engagement within the organization?

21. I am working on best practices for maintaining employee records in Broken Arrow, Oklahoma. What are the recommended methods for accurate and secure record-keeping?

22. I am working on updating and improving the employee handbook in Edmond, Oklahoma. Can you suggest ways to make the employee handbook more informative and effective?

23. I am working on identifying cost-effective employee benefits in Joplin, Missouri. What benefits can we offer to employees that are both cost-effective and valuable?

24. I am working on a method for calculating the ROI on employee training programs in Chesterfield, Missouri. How can we measure the return on investment for our training initiatives?

25. I am working on improving internal communications within the organization in St. Joseph, Missouri. How can we enhance communication and collaboration among employees and departments?

26. I am working on strategies for addressing employee grievances effectively in Lakeville, Minnesota. What approaches can we use to handle employee grievances with fairness and efficiency?

27. What are some wellness initiatives that could improve employee health and productivity?

28. Propose a strategy for ongoing professional development for

employees.

29. How can we incorporate employee feedback into HR policy?

30. Suggest approaches to make orientation programs more engaging and informative.

31. What are the considerations for managing employee benefits like pensions and retirement plans?

32. I am working on preparing employees for leadership roles in Stillwater, Oklahoma. What development programs or initiatives can help employees develop leadership skills?

33. I am working on effective retention strategies for high-performing employees in Lawton, Oklahoma. What measures can be implemented to retain and motivate high-performing talent?

34. How can we engage employees in corporate social responsibility initiatives?

35. I am working on maintaining high employee morale in Key West, Florida. Can you describe strategies for keeping morale high during challenging times?

36. I am working on employee mentoring and coaching plans in Boca Raton, Florida. Can you propose an effective plan for mentoring and coaching?

37. I am working on ensuring alignment of employees with the organization's values and mission in Amarillo, Texas. How can we achieve this alignment?

38. I am working on increasing employee satisfaction surveys' response rates in Tallahassee, Florida. What are effective ways to boost response rates?

39. I am working on HR's support for employees during organizational changes in Sarasota, Florida. How can HR best support employees in times of change?

40. I am working on legal considerations in employee terminations in Corpus Christi, Texas. What legal aspects should

we be aware of during termination?

41. I am working on managing employee time-off and leave policies in Homestead, Florida. How can we manage this effectively?

42. I am working on adapting HR policies for international or culturally diverse employees in Amarillo, Texas. What considerations are important for this adaptation?

43. I am working on HR's support for the mental health of employees in Naples, Florida. How can HR contribute to mental health support?

44. I am working on considerations for employees during mergers or acquisitions in Cocoa Beach, Florida. What should we consider during such transitions?

45. I am working on addressing the challenges of employee burnout in Tyler, Texas. How can we tackle employee burnout effectively?

46. I am working on better managing overtime and its impact on employees in Wichita Falls, Texas. How can we manage overtime effectively?

47. I am working on the key components of an effective employee assistance program in Victoria, Texas. What are these key components?

48. I am working on HR strategies in Albuquerque. How can HR ensure that employee skills stay up to date in a rapidly changing environment?

49. I am working on improving employee orientation for seasonal or temporary hires in Alamogordo. How can we enhance employee orientation for such hires?

50. I am working on methods to encourage volunteerism among employees in Clovis. Can you suggest effective methods?

51. I am working on managing employee performance in a matrix

organization in Sunland Park. Can you describe effective strategies for this?

52. I am working on HR strategies for job rotations and cross-training in Wilmington. How can HR effectively manage job rotations and cross-training to benefit our organization?

53. I am working on employee development in Wilmington. How can we best prepare our employees for transitions into managerial roles?

54. I am working on HR policies for retired employees in Dover. What considerations should we keep in mind when bringing back retired employees for part-time or consultancy roles?

55. I am working on skills development initiatives in Dover. Can you suggest a comprehensive plan for updating employee skills to keep up with technological advancements?

56. I am working on employee wellness initiatives in Cincinnati. What are some ways to incorporate employee wellness into the organizational culture?

57. What are some methods for training civilians in emergency preparedness in Dayton?

58. I am working on recruitment and training strategies for emergency responders in Yonkers. Could you describe a recruitment and training strategy that would help us enhance our emergency response capabilities?

59. I am a First Aid Training Manager working in Pinecrest. Please help me explore how we can improve first aid training among the public.

60. I am a Soft Skills Trainer working in Hillside. Please help me explore training programs to improve the soft skills of public safety personnel.

61. I am a Training Coordinator working on fostering a culture of continuous learning among development services staff in Watertown. Please help me describe training programs,

knowledge sharing platforms, and professional development opportunities that promote ongoing learning and skill enhancement within our team.

62. I am working on crisis and emergency response planning for the city of Grand Rapids' parks. Please help me identify strategies for effective crisis and emergency response, including communication systems, evacuation plans, and safety training for park staff and visitors.

63. What training programs can be put in place to align staff skills with strategic goals?

64. I am the Human Resources Director for the city of Houston. Please help me discuss strategies for talent management to meet the future needs of our city's operations.

65. You're the Emergency Medical Services (EMS) Training Coordinator based in Chesapeake. Share how you would develop and implement training programs for EMS personnel.

66. Imagine you're the Workers' Compensation Coordinator in Cary. Describe your role in managing workers' compensation claims, including ensuring injured employees receive appropriate care and benefits while controlling costs for the city.

POLICY & LEGISLATION

67. I am a city administrator, please tell me what I can do to make this agreement better. I am particularly concerned about potential risks and liabilities from this Intergovernmental Agreement. What language can be added to help?

68. Please analyze the following city policy for clarity, conciseness, and assess to make sure we didnt miss anything.

69. I am a City Manager looking to update my city code on the hours of operation for our park. Right now, the park is open 7 days a week from 7am-12am. We want to update the hours to 7am-10pm on M-TH, and 7am-11pm on Fri-Sun. Please draft an ordinance that Council can pass to amend the city code.

70. Write an ordinance permitting up to 2 chickens in a residential home in broken arrow, ok. This applies only to single family residences, and not multi-family dwellings.

71. You are a virtual EOC in an Emergency Operations Center in ___, AZ. We are doing an exercise. Use the Phoenix Fire Department SOP Volume 2 as your guide for deployment of resources on fire related incidents, and use NIMS and ICS for incident management. We have 4 fire stations (Station 1 at [address]; Station 2 at [address]; Station 3 at [address]; Station 4 at [address]) each station has an Engine truck (E1 at station 1, E2 at Station 2, etc.), except Station 4, which has a ladder truck (L4). There is a battalion truck for the Battalion Chief. And we also have 1 reserve truck (E11). The police department is located at 100 W.

Main Street. At any given time, there are 5 patrol officers on duty, plus a sergeant and a lieutenant. The city is part of an Automatic Aid Agreement. The Police Dispatch is PSAP but transfers medical and fire calls to Phoenix Fire Dispatch, because Phoenix dispatches our fire. The fire department handles all fire and medical calls. As the virtual EOC you will function as each ESF. When responding, you will let me know what ESF you are reporting as. Now let's run a table talk exercise.

72. Our city council is considering implementing a new policy to reduce traffic congestion. Please provide the pros and cons of this policy. What are the potential benefits and drawbacks of implementing this policy?

73. Tell me the federal laws, statutes, and policies that relate to ground ambulance services. link to sources

74. Turn this discipline policy into a flow chart, so I can help my first-line supervisors visualize the steps they need to take.

75. Give me an analysis of this proposed policy. I want to know the 2nd and 3rd order effects:

76. Use the following to help me understand how to create a municipal budget for a city in Tennessee https://comptroller.tn.gov/office-functions/lgf/budgets/municipalities.html https://comptroller.tn.gov/content/dam/cot/lgf/documents/budgets/cities/2024MunicipalBudgetMemo.pdf https://comptroller.tn.gov/content/dam/cot/lgf/documents/budgets/cities/2024SampleMunicipalBudgetOrdinance.pdf https://comptroller.tn.gov/content/dam/cot/lgf/documents/budgets/cities/2024MunicipalBudgetSubmissionChecklist.pdf https://comptroller.tn.gov/content/dam/cot/lgf/documents/templates/BudgetSchedules2024.xlsx https://comptroller.tn.gov/content/dam/cot/lgf/documents/budgets/cities/2024SampleMunicipalBudgetOrdinance.docx https://comptroller.tn.gov/content/dam/cot/lgf/documents/budgets/cities/CertificationTemplateMunicipality.docx

77. [upload public sector workforce data from the US Census Bureau] Give me some recommendations for analysis if I am a policy analyst with the State of Michigan

78. Please provide a bulleted summary of the responsibilities for both parties in the agreement

79. Meeting or exceeding federal and state regulations is a top priority. Can you share strategies that guarantee all our projects consistently adhere to and even surpass the necessary regulatory requirements?

80. Staying updated on evolving construction codes and standards is vital. Could you present a comprehensive strategy for keeping our department well-informed about the latest developments in construction regulations and best practices?

81. Imagine you're the Compliance Assurance Specialist based in Oakridge Vista. Suggest effective ways to ensure compliance with federal and state financial regulations within the municipality.

82. As the Financial Metrics Tracking Consultant in Elmwood Park, propose methods to better track and report on financial metrics, ensuring compliance with regulations.

83. I am working on improving compliance with labor laws and regulations in Minnetonka, Minnesota. What measures and practices can help us maintain compliance with labor regulations?

84. I am a Community Policing Advisor working in Sunville. Please help me discuss how we can engage communities in dialogue about policing and law enforcement.

85. I am working on code compliance and enforcement for the city of Greenbelt. Please help me explore how we can enhance code compliance and enforcement efforts, ensuring that developments align with city regulations and standards.

86. I am a Management Analyst working on strategies for reducing noise pollution in Aberdeen. Please help me identify

methods such as noise barriers, soundproofing, and zoning regulations to mitigate noise pollution in urban areas.

87. In Council Bluffs, we make swimming areas safer and cleaner by increasing lifeguard presence, implementing regular water quality testing, offering swim lessons, and promoting a "pack it in, pack it out" policy for park visitors to reduce litter.

88. I am a Tax Policy Analyst for the city of Charlotte. Please help me explore how we can optimize tax policy to stimulate economic development in our city.

89. I am the Zoning Adaptation Planner for the city of Wichita. Please help me explore how zoning laws can be adapted to encourage economic growth and development in our city.

90. I am the Business Regulations Manager for the city of Atlanta. Please help me discuss how the government can streamline regulatory procedures to make it easier for businesses to operate.

91. I am a Social Services Director for ___ County. Homelessness is a complex issue that requires a multi-pronged approach. Help me identify strategies to address homelessness in the community. How can I approach homelessness from a policy and implementation perspective?

92. Assume the position of Transit Safety Compliance Officer in Tuscaloosa. Share strategies for ensuring compliance with safety regulations and standards in our transit operations.

93. Imagine you're the Fire Inspector in Norfolk. Discuss methods for ensuring compliance with fire safety regulations in commercial and residential properties.

FINANCE & BUDGETING

94. I am the finance director of a city, and I am being asked to give a presentation to my local chamber of commerce. Please give me 3 ideas for the presentation, which will last about 20 minutes.

95. You are budgetGPT. Walk me through how to build a municipal budget.

96. What insights can you give me from this budget:

97. I am a city administrator in the city of ____. Please help me do a historical trend analysis on state shared revenue funds for my city.

98. I am a city manager of ____. please create a gfoa budget memo based on information from the following source. This is for the FY23 budget. direct the memo to the mayor and council of Center, Texas. I am the city manager.

99. I am a City Manager of Wichita Falls TX. I need to create a budget memo to accompany the FY23 budget. please create the memo in gfoa format. Include the fulling information: This budget will raise more revenue from property taxes than last year's budget by an amount of $1,448,300, which is a 3.49% increase from last year's budget. The property tax revenue to be raised from new property added to the tax roll this year is $649,442.

100. I'm an accountant for the city of ____. I need to write an SOP for bank reconciliation that is compliant with the Government Finance Officers Association guidelines. Please provide me with a

step-by-step SOP which complies with standard internal controls for a municipality.

101. What insights can you gather from this budget:

102. Draft a budget cover letter

103. Create a line chart showing the year of year increase of each tax revenue fund [upload 2 or more years of budget spreadsheets]

104. What taxes have the highest change in percentage since 2021? [upload 2 or more years of budget spreadsheets]

105. Recommend 3 visualizations for this expenditures report [upload spreadsheet]. for context, I am a city manager and im interested in learning how i can manage this budget more efficiently and effectively.

106. Give me 3 actionable ways for the finance department to contribute to each part of this strategic plan: [insert link to strategic plan]

107. I am a City Manager of Wichita Falls, TX. I need to create a budget memo to accompany the FY2023 budget. Please create the memo in a format that complies with GFOA standards for municipal budgeting.

108. Please create a multi-line chart with each state-shared revenue fund being a different colored line

109. I am a finance director in Ketchikan AK. I want to do some revenue forecasting analysis from the 2021, 2022, 2023 budget. Below are the budgets in order for the year.

110. You are the finance director for the city of ___. Propose a strategy for efficient budget allocation.

111. You are a budget manager for the city of ___. Identify potential areas for cost-cutting without affecting public services.

112. I am the budget manager for the city of ___. How can we make the annual budget process more transparent?

113. I am a grants analyst for ___ County. Describe a grant-writing strategy to secure more funding.

114. I am a public works director. How can we make the best use of limited public works budgets?

115. I am a CIP analyst in the finance department in the city of ___. What metrics can be used to evaluate the ROI of infrastructure projects?

116. How can we make the annual budgeting process more efficient?

117. In your role as Public Engagement Coordinator in Rivertown Junction, suggest effective methods to actively involve public input in budget decisions.

118. Imagine you're the Budget Alignment Manager in Brookside Haven. Share your insights on how we can better align the budget with our municipality's strategic goals.

119. In your role as Transparency Initiative Coordinator in Maplewood Fields, propose an initiative to significantly increase budget transparency in our municipality.

120. As the Real-time Budget Tracking Solutions Manager in Clearwater Pines, present a digital solution for real-time budget tracking, ensuring transparency and accountability.

121. Describe a plan for maximizing the impact of grant funding.

122. How can we improve collaboration with non-profits and private companies for additional funding?

123. Suggest ways to manage and refinance existing loans more effectively.

124. How can we achieve a balanced budget while paying down debt?

125. You're the Emergency Fund Size Advisor in Brookside Haven. Share insights into determining an appropriate size for an emergency fund tailored to our municipality's needs.

126. In your role as the Contingency Fund Manager in Redwood Springs, describe a strategy for accumulating and maintaining a contingency fund to ensure financial resilience.

127. As the Emergency Fund Allocation Strategist in Oakridge Pines, suggest criteria for the allocation of emergency funds to different municipal needs.

128. What is the best strategy for managing pension funds and other post-employment benefits?

129. How should we prioritize large capital projects in the budget?

130. Propose a funding mechanism for multi-year capital projects.

131. How can we improve project budget tracking for capital expenditures?

132. Propose methods to educate the public about the municipal budget.

133. Suggest strategies for handling public criticism about budget decisions.

134. What are some effective ways to present budget information in public meetings?

135. Describe a strategy for allocating funds for environmental initiatives.

136. How can we incorporate performance-based budgeting?

137. How can we protect municipal finances from volatile economic conditions?

138. What is the role of economic forecasting in budget planning?

139. How can the budget be adjusted to respond to changes in federal and state financial policies?

140. I am working on budget allocation for public safety in the city of Syracuse. What are some cost-effective enhancements we can make to improve public safety?

141. In Des Moines, we explore alternative revenue streams

for parks beyond public funding by implementing sponsorship and naming rights programs, hosting fundraising events, and exploring partnerships with local businesses for advertising and concessions.

142. I am a finance analyst for the city of Indianapolis. Please help me outline steps to improve local residents' financial literacy, ultimately empowering them to make informed economic decisions.

143. I am the Business Grants Advisor for the city of Chicago. Please help me explain how we can assist local businesses in obtaining various forms of grants and funding.

144. I am the Fundraising Manager for the library system in Baxter County. Please help me explore strategies that can be used to fundraise for our libraries.

145. What strategies can be used to maintain and increase library funding?

146. How can you ensure that the budget aligns with strategic objectives?

147. I am the Grants Coordinator for the city of Denver. Please help me develop strategies for securing grants and other external funding to support strategic initiatives.

OPERATIONS & MAINTENANCE

148. I am an emergency manager for _____. We just experienced a wildfire and there is an imminent threat of post-fire flooding. We want to host a community meeting that outlines the steps taken by the proper authorities to contain the fire while also preparing individuals for the potential of flooding. We want to discuss evacuation procedures and steps the city and local jurisdictions are taking to mitigate the effects of potential flooding, as well as ways the community can help. We also want to provide resources for those impacted and help people know what resources are available. Please help me draft the agenda for this community meeting.

149. Please help me create a survey that enables me to identify vulnerable populations who may be impacted most by flooding, and I also want to know if individuals/households have been impacted by the wildfire and whether they have been able to secure adequate resources or if they even know that resources exist to help and support during a disaster. Please also provide the survey in Spanish

150. I am a Town Manager in ___. We just experienced post-fire flooding and I want to do a community survey to assess the needs and also understand whether residents have accessed resources, and if they are aware of available resources. Also provide a Spanish language translation for residents from Mexico.

151. I'm thinking of effective and efficient staffing and operational

models for the Park Rangers team. Below are some of my thoughts. Please help guide my analysis and give me some further questions for further research and analysis.

152. The Community Resources department for the city of _____ is facing budget constraints while planning a community event. Please suggest alternative solutions that can help us organize a successful event within the budget. What are some creative and cost-effective ways to make the event successful with limited resources?

153. Write a memo from a Fire Chief requesting CIP funds to purchase pre-emption devices on 3 fire engines. preemption devices allow fire apparatuses to change traffic light signals and allow vehicles to safely and quickly arrive on scene. This device can save up to 15-30 seconds per intersection. The cost of this device is 10,000 per vehicle with an annual maintenance contract of 2,500 per year.

154. Give me 5-10 non-traditional org chart models for a city fire department, which emphasize operational efficiency

155. Create a budget presentation for the Gila County Board of Supervisors based on this budget (https://www.gilacountyaz.gov/2023%20Tentative%20Budget%20-%20Schedules%20A-G.pdf). Show how the budget aligns to the strategic plan (https://www.gilacountyaz.gov/Strategic%20Plan%202019%20PDF.pdf). Include graphs using the data from the budget. Use only information from those pdfs. no placeholders

156. I am a Tax Analyst working on optimizing revenue streams for the city of Allentown. Analyze the impact of recent property tax reforms on municipal revenue. Provide a report that includes year-over-year comparisons, identifies trends, and recommends adjustments for future tax policies to ensure fiscal sustainability.

157. I am the City Manager for Scranton, focusing on overall operational efficiency and community satisfaction. Evaluate the performance metrics of each city department over the last fiscal

year. Based on this data, formulate a strategic plan to improve services, reduce costs, and enhance public engagement for the upcoming year.

158. I am a streets manager for the city of ___. Describe plans for winter road maintenance.

159. I am a facilities manager for the city of __. Outline a preventive maintenance schedule for public buildings.

160. I am the Parks Rangers Supervisor for the city of ___. How can we improve the maintenance and safety of public parks?

161. What new technologies can be employed for more efficient road maintenance?

162. I am the fleet manager for ___ county. How can we improve maintenance schedules for public vehicles?

163. As the Resource Allocation Strategist in Meadowbrook, outline a comprehensive strategy for a more equitable allocation of resources within our municipality.

164. As the Asset Income Generation Specialist in Clearwater Valley, suggest ways to generate income through asset leasing or selling while maximizing the municipality's resources.

165. I am working on implementing flexible work schedules in Norman, Oklahoma. Can you describe effective methods for introducing and managing flexible work arrangements?

166. I am working on improving collaboration between HR and other departments in Joplin, Missouri. What strategies can be employed to enhance cooperation and communication between HR and other teams?

167. I am working on data security measures in HR operations in Roswell. How can we ensure data security in HR operations?

168. I am an Interagency Cooperation Coordinator working in Greenfield. Please help me describe ways to enhance cooperation between local and federal safety agencies.

169. I am a Mental Health Support Coordinator working in Harmonyville. Please help me suggest a plan for increasing the mental health resources for public safety personnel.

170. I am working on legal considerations in public safety for Greenville County, SC. Please help me discuss the legal considerations in public safety operations.

171. I am working on Small Business Support for Sheboygan County, WI. Please help me explore how we can facilitate local small business growth in Sheboygan County, including access to resources, financial support, and networking opportunities.

172. I am working on small business support for Allegheny County. Please help me explore how we can facilitate local small business growth in Allegheny County, including access to resources, financial support, and networking opportunities.

173. I am an Innovation Manager working on a plan for developing incubators or innovation hubs in Watertown. Please help me outline the design, resources, and programs that will support entrepreneurship, innovation, and business growth within our community.

174. I am working on innovative ways to fund park development and maintenance in Memphis. Please help me explore strategies such as public-private partnerships, sponsorships, crowdfunding, and grant applications to secure funding for our parks.

175. I am working on ensuring the longevity of park trees and plant life for the city of Flint. Please help me explore ways to care for and protect park trees and plant life, including tree maintenance, pest control, and biodiversity promotion.

176. I am working on volunteer engagement in park maintenance for the city of Dearborn. Please help me outline a strategy for actively involving community volunteers in park maintenance, organizing cleanup events, tree planting initiatives, and other projects to enhance our parks collaboratively.

177. In Waterloo, we describe a plan for a new dog park, including features such as separate areas for small and large dogs, agility equipment, waste disposal stations, regular maintenance schedules, and clear rules for responsible dog ownership.

178. In Madison, we employ strategies for maintaining cleanliness in busy urban parks by implementing regular cleaning schedules, increasing the number of waste disposal bins, and engaging community volunteers in clean-up initiatives to keep our parks pristine.

179. I am the Parks Director in Kenosha working on improving safety measures for our parks. Conduct a risk assessment template to help identify potential safety hazards like poorly lit areas, lack of signage, or damaged equipment. Develop a prioritized action plan to address these issues and consider the feasibility of community watch programs.

180. In Papillion, we host revenue-generating events in parks such as concerts, outdoor movie nights, and food festivals, generating income to support park maintenance and improvements.

181. In La Vista, we have implemented a park "Adopt-a-Tree" and "Adopt-a-Bench" program, allowing community members and organizations to contribute to park beautification and maintenance efforts.

182. In Lexington, we use parks for community education on sustainability by organizing workshops, nature hikes, and educational programs that highlight environmental conservation and responsible resource use.

183. I am the Maintenance Schedule Optimization Manager for the city of Augusta. Please help me outline methods for optimizing maintenance schedules in our parks to minimize disruption to visitors while ensuring their upkeep.

184. I am the Public-Private Partnership Facilitator for the city of Spokane. Please help me explain how public-private partnerships can contribute to economic growth by combining resources and

expertise.

185. I am the Gig Economy Support Specialist for the city of Nashville. Please help me discuss ways in which we can support the gig economy, providing opportunities and resources for independent workers in our mid-sized city.

186. I am the Natural Resource Sustainability Advisor for the city of Oklahoma City. Please help me outline a responsible strategy to leverage our local natural resources for economic benefit while ensuring long-term sustainability and environmental stewardship.

187. I am the Innovation Strategy Officer for the city of Austin. Please help me brainstorm ways to foster innovation within the public sector and drive progress in our city's services and operations.

188. I am the Digital Services Manager for the city of San Francisco. Please help me describe a comprehensive plan for an "open for business" portal to facilitate business operations in the city.

189. Describe a plan to increase digital literacy through library resources.

190. Discuss the potential for libraries to serve as emergency shelters or resource centers.

191. I am the Financial Literacy Program Director for the library system in Gibson County. Please help me describe a program for teaching financial literacy using our library resources.

192. Discuss ways to provide mental health resources through the library.

193. Discuss partnerships with other libraries for sharing resources.

194. What are some ways to offer virtual events or resources for those who cannot visit the library?

195. I am the Chief Technology Officer for the city of San Jose. Please help me describe how we can use technology to improve operational efficiency across all departments.

196. I am the Resource Allocation Specialist for the city of New Orleans. Please help me discuss strategies for allocating resources in a manner that supports our strategic plan.

197. I am the Director of Environmental Services for the city of Portland. Please help me outline how we can incorporate principles of the circular economy into city operations for sustainability and reduced waste.

198. I am a deputy city manager, and I am Implementing a performance review system aligned with strategic goals that can significantly impact the effectiveness and efficiency of city or county operations. Detail the steps I should take to establish a performance review system that aligns with the strategic goals of the city or county. How can I design and implement a performance review system to ensure that it aligns closely with the city's or county's strategic goals?

199. I work in Finance for the City of ___. Funding for infrastructure maintenance is often limited but crucial. Discuss ways to secure funding for infrastructure maintenance. Recommend strategies to secure adequate funding for ongoing infrastructure maintenance.

200. Imagine you're the Transit Maintenance Supervisor in Huntsville. Describe a plan for proactive maintenance to ensure the longevity and safety of our transit fleet.

201. As the Emergency Manager in Wilmington, outline your approach to developing and maintaining effective emergency response plans, including coordination with various agencies, community outreach, and resource allocation to ensure the city's preparedness for unforeseen crises and disasters.

RISK MANAGEMENT

202. I am evaluating the following business case. Help me evaluate and identify 2nd and 3rd order effects, possible risks, and the overall logic of the business case.

203. i want you to tell me all of the unintended consequences and risks about this idea

204. You're the Investment Risk Assessment Analyst in Brookside Harbor. Explain how to evaluate the risk and return of various investment options for the municipality.

205. Assume the position of Revenue Stream Predictability Analyst in Cedarwood Vista. Discuss how to improve the predictability and reliability of revenue streams for better budget planning.

206. What are some risk mitigation strategies for capital projects?

207. I am working on risk assessment for public safety in the city of Buffalo. Could you suggest a method to assess and manage risks in our public safety planning?

208. I am the Risk Management Officer for the city of Salt Lake City. Please help me identify the risks associated with our strategic plan and how these risks will be mitigated.

209. I am the Legal Counsel for the city of Dallas. Please help me discuss the role of legal compliance in strategic planning to ensure that all initiatives are above board and minimize risks.

210. I am a member of the Flood Control District. Please help me identify strategies for flood prevention and management that can

help to mitigate flood risks and manage flood events effectively.

211. As the Transit Operations Manager in Birmingham, suggest strategies to improve the punctuality and reliability of public transportation services.

212. As the Risk Manager in Asheville, outline your strategy for identifying, assessing, and mitigating risks within the city's operations and services.

213. You're the Insurance Analyst in Durham. Explain your role in analyzing insurance policies, negotiating coverage terms, and ensuring cost-effective risk coverage for the city.

ECONOMIC DEVELOPMENT

214. I am an economic development director for _____. Please give me some ideas on how I can use ChatGPT in my job.

215. Draft an economic development plan for the city of ____

216. I am the economic development director for lavergne tn. help me analyze these pdfs on the area demographics of lavergne and the implications to economic development

217. I am an economic development analyst for the southeast wisconsin region. please summarize these two comprehensive plans and give me insights on regional economic development opportunities from these two documents:

218. Please describe if there are any overlaps or economic development opportunities in this 5 year plan: [insert link to 5 year plan].

219. please describe if there are any overlaps or economic development opportunities from this planning document

220. I am the downtown economic development manager for the city of ___. Propose an initiative to restore neglected historical buildings.

221. I am the Economic Development Director for the City of ___. How can we attract new businesses to our area?

222. I am an economic development management analyst. Suggest ways to support local entrepreneurs.

223. I am an economic development manager for ___ county. List potential areas for commercial development.

224. I am an economic development analyst for ___ county. How can we encourage local tourism?

225. I am working on Economic Development for Coconino County, AZ. Please help me examine how local development can contribute to job creation in Coconino County, including industry diversification, workforce development, and entrepreneurship support.

226. I am working on economic development for Miami-Dade County. Please help me examine how local development can contribute to job creation in Miami-Dade County, including industry diversification, workforce development, and entrepreneurship support.

227. I am an Economic Development Specialist working on facilitating the growth of local artisan and craft industries for the city of Naperville. Please help me identify ways to support and promote local artisans, such as craft fairs, incubator spaces, and marketing initiatives.

228. I am the Sustainable Economic Development Planner for the city of Santa Barbara. Please help me outline the key components of our sustainable economic development plan, ensuring long-term prosperity while considering environmental and social factors.

229. I am the Educational Institutions Liaison for Economic Development for the city of Eugene. Please help me explain the important role that educational institutions play in driving economic development through research, innovation, and workforce development.

230. I am the Economic Impact Measurement Analyst for the city of Greenville. Please help me describe how to measure the impact of economic development initiatives accurately, providing valuable insights for our local government.

231. I am the Climate Change Economic Analyst for the city of Burlington. Please help me discuss the impact of climate change on economic development and strategies for resilience in our mid-sized city.

232. I am the Healthcare Economic Development Advisor for the city of Olympia. Please help me explore the critical role healthcare plays in economic development in our mid-sized city.

233. I am the Business Summit Planning Director for the city of Lexington. Please help me describe a plan for an annual business summit that brings together key stakeholders, fosters networking, and promotes economic development within our mid-sized city.

234. I am an Economic Development analyst for the city of Albuquerque. Please help me explore how we can balance economic development with environmental conservation in our city.

235. I am the Citizen Engagement Officer for the city of Omaha. Please help me identify ways to engage citizens actively in economic development planning and decision-making processes.

236. I am an Economic Development Manager focusing on Niche Market Development for the city of Tulsa. Please help me discuss the potential of niche markets like craft breweries or eco-tourism and how they can contribute to our city's economic diversity.

237. I am an Economic Development Analyst for the city of Minneapolis. Please help me discuss effective ways to foster a vibrant startup culture within our city, encouraging innovation and economic growth.

238. I am the Sports and Entertainment Economic Development Specialist for the city of Raleigh. Please help me explore how we can leverage sports and entertainment events to generate economic gains and enhance our city's profile.

239. I am the Talent Acquisition Specialist for the city of

Albuquerque. Please help me explore ways to engage with local college alumni networks strategically for the purpose of economic development in our city.

240. I am an Economic Development Director for the city of Memphis. Please help me outline strategies to foster growth and innovation in our local food and beverage sector, driving economic development.

241. I am an Economic Development Analyst for the city of Boise. Please help me explore methods to attract film and TV productions to our city, enhancing our local economy and creative industry.

242. I am the Economic Development Manager for the city of Raleigh. Please help me outline our strategy for seasonal economic development to maximize opportunities and growth throughout the year.

243. I am the Transportation Logistics Coordinator for the city of Tulsa. Please help me explain the significance of transportation logistics in driving economic development in the city.

244. I am an Economic Development Analyst focusing on small business support in the city of ___. Recommend 5 ways that I can support local small businesses?

245. I am an Economic Development Director for the city of ___. Please help me develop a set of initiatives aimed at boosting local tourism and attracting visitors to positively impact the local economy.

GENERAL

246. I am the Town Manager of ____. I want to apply for a CDBG grant to increase the roadwidth in our downtown area to accommodate a bike lane. The downtown consists of a 3-mile stretch, and I want the bike lane to go in both directions.

247. According to the MUCTC what are the requirements for an intersection to have a four-way traffic light

248. You are GrantApplicantGPT. I want you to help the Town of ____ apply for a CBDG grant.

249. summarize this into one paragraph:

250. You are a 911 dispatch manager. Create a staffing model for 3 supervisors and 10 dispatchers that allows them to work 4 10hr days.

251. Tell me everything that could go wrong or is unsustainable in this proposal:

252. Make the following sound more concise and friendlier

253. Please read this document and then provide recommendations for analysis

254. Put the following into a comprehensive and succinct sentence. Reword if necessary.

255. Do nothing just acknowledge

256. What are the functional distinctions in the 3 job descriptions?

257. Here are 4 different facebook posts. i want you to give me

overall themes and perspectives from the comments on these posts: [Insert links to posts]

258. Create a word cloud of the most common words and phrases in this post: [insert link to post]

259. Create a 10-slide presentation from this source:

260. Reword the following:

261. You are a data analyst. Compare and contrast the demographics of traffic stops in these reports.

262. Teach me how to construct the perfect prompt. Include a template prompt structure.

263. You are a municipal data analyst. build some graphs that help give deep insights into this dataset.

264. Generate a weather threat matrix for the July 4th event in ___, zip code ___. The event will take place from 5:00pm to 9:00pm, and we expect 10,000 guests.

265. Use these bullets to draft a cohesive and succinct paragraph

266. [upload public sector workforce data from the US Census Bureau] Give me the top 5 highest total payrolls by government function in Michigan

267. give me 3 ways to analyze this data

268. create a presentation from this

269. please give an overview and summary of this page:

270. Please suggest a forecasting model based on this data

271. Please suggest 4 visualizations to best analyze and understand this data

272. please use the following notes to draft a memo on ___ topic to ___ recipient(s)

273. please put the following into a word document I can download

274. Please help me put these thoughts together in a more cohesive and comprehensive way.

275. I am the Assistant County Manager in ____. Describe how to make municipal data more accessible to the public.

276. I am the procurement analyst for ___. Describe a strategy for cost-effective procurement of materials and equipment.

277. Suggest ways to manage traffic congestion during school hours.

278. How can we improve road signage for better traffic flow?

279. Describe how to conduct a comprehensive inventory of municipal assets.

280. As the Revenue Diversification Specialist based in Forest Grove, proposes innovative ways to diversify our revenue streams.

281. You're the Financial Communication Director in Pinecrest Valley. Describe a plan to make financial reports more understandable and accessible to the general public.

282. As the Internal Financial Reporting Specialist in Cedarwood Bluffs, describe methods and processes to enhance our internal financial reporting mechanisms for better decision-making.

283. Describe a plan for systematic cost analysis across all departments.

284. How can we reduce energy costs in municipal buildings?

285. Suggest ways to streamline procurement to achieve savings.

286. Propose a strategy for identifying and applying for federal and state grants.

287. What are the pros and cons of short-term vs. long-term borrowing?

288. In your role as the Internal Financial Review Coordinator in Redwood Glen, detail the steps to conduct a thorough internal financial review.

289. Imagine you're the Asset Safeguarding Coordinator in Pinecrest Fields. Share strategies on how to safeguard municipal assets effectively.

290. Imagine you're the Financial Resilience Coordinator in Silverwood Meadows. Discuss how to improve financial resilience in the face of unexpected events.

291. Suggest methods for automating payroll to reduce errors.

292. What are the financial considerations when entering into a public-private partnership?

293. How can we structure contracts to protect municipal interests?

294. Suggest a framework for financial reporting in public-private partnerships.

295. What is the role of contingency planning in these partnerships?

296. How can artificial intelligence be used for financial analysis and forecasting?

297. How can we use social media to increase transparency around financial matters?

298. Propose methods for quantifying the financial impact of sustainable practices.

299. How can we use performance metrics to identify areas for cost savings?

300. Describe strategies for avoiding cost overruns in contracts.

301. Describe contingency plans for economic downturns.

302. Suggest ways to make performance evaluations more effective.

303. I am working on methods for better conflict resolution in the workplace in Independence, Missouri. How can we enhance conflict resolution processes for a more harmonious workplace?

304. I am working on better utilizing part-time and temporary workers in Stillwater, Oklahoma. What methods can we use to effectively integrate part-time and temporary staff into our workforce?

305. How can we adapt HR practices to accommodate remote work?

306. How can HR metrics and KPIs be better tracked and analyzed?

307. Suggest measures for reducing absenteeism and tardiness.

308. How can we improve our internship and apprenticeship programs?

309. I am working on potential applications for AI and automation in HR in Eden Prairie, Minnesota. How can we leverage AI and automation to streamline HR processes and enhance efficiency?

310. I am working on a process for regularly updating job descriptions in O'Fallon, Missouri. What steps can we take to ensure that job descriptions remain accurate and up to date?

311. I am working on adapting HR strategies to meet seasonal staffing needs in Eagan, Minnesota. How can HR effectively plan and manage staffing fluctuations during seasonal periods?

312. I am working on the keys to effective negotiation in labor relations in Burnsville, Minnesota. What strategies and skills are essential for successful negotiations in labor relations?

313. I am working on considerations for allowing pets in the workplace in El Paso, Texas. What should we consider when implementing such policies?

314. I am working on methods to ensure fairness in bonuses and incentives in Fort Myers, Florida. Can you suggest ways to achieve fairness?

315. I am working on managing the integration of new technologies into the workplace in St. Petersburg, Florida. What

steps should be taken to manage this integration?

316. I am working on improving the grievance reporting mechanism in Gainesville, Florida. How can we enhance this mechanism?

317. I am working on recognizing and celebrating organizational milestones in Abilene, Texas. Can you describe a plan for this?

318. I am working on leveraging HR data analytics for strategic planning in Delray Beach, Florida. How can HR data analytics be used strategically?

319. I am working on conflict prevention techniques in Santa Fe. Can you suggest effective ways to prevent conflicts in a diverse work environment?

320. I am working on best practices for managing remote and hybrid teams in Farmington. Can you suggest some best practices?

321. Please use the following notes to draft a memo for Dayton.

322. What are some strategies for natural disaster preparedness in Cincinnati?

323. How can we better manage crowd control during public events in Dayton?

324. What are some best practices for data-driven policing in Akron?

325. Suggest strategies for reducing domestic violence incidents in Cincinnati.

326. What are some preventative measures to reduce petty crime in Dublin?

327. Suggest ways to improve the effectiveness of neighborhood watch programs in Cincinnati.

328. Describe strategies for increasing public awareness about cyber threats in Dayton.

329. I am a Hazardous Material Preparedness Coordinator

working in Hillside. Please help me suggest a plan for hazardous material incident preparedness.

330. I am a Crime Reduction Strategist working at Lakeside. Please help me consider long-term strategies for reducing crime rates.

331. I am a Public Warning System Manager working in Riverdale. Please help me suggest improvements for the public warning system.

332. I am a Counter-Terrorism Planner working in Riverdale. Please help me describe a strategy for counter-terrorism preparedness.

333. I am a DUI Prevention Advocate working in Willowbrook. Please help me consider how we can reduce the incidence of DUI and drunk driving.

334. I am a Human Trafficking Prevention Coordinator working in Pinecrest. Please help me consider measures for combating human trafficking.

335. I am a Gang Violence Reduction Strategist working in Lakeside. Please help me explore strategies for reducing gang violence.

336. I am a Mass Casualty Response Planner working in Riverdale. Please help me explore how we can ensure effective medical responses in mass casualty incidents.

337. I am a Mass Casualty Response Planner working in Riverdale. Please help me explore how we can ensure effective medical responses.

338. I am working on crisis communication for Salt Lake County, UT. Please help me describe a strategy for effective crisis communication.

339. I am working on transparency in criminal investigations for Fayette County, KY. Please help me describe methods for improving the transparency of criminal investigations.

340. What role can libraries play in early childhood education?

341. Describe methods for curating an inclusive book selection that represents diverse perspectives.

342. Describe a strategy for managing and promoting an eBook collection.

343. Describe strategies for providing career counseling and resume-building workshops.

344. Discuss the challenges and solutions for inter-departmental collaboration.

345. What are some KPIs that can measure the success of the strategic plan?

346. I am the Director of Continuous Improvement for Jefferson County. Please help me develop methods to foster a culture of continuous improvement across all departments.

347. I am the Objectives Coordinator for Franklin County. Please help me describe a framework for setting both short-term and long-term objectives in our strategic planning.

348. I am the Stakeholder Engagement Manager for Washington County. Please help me outline ways to engage external stakeholders in our strategic planning process.

349. I am the Data Analytics Officer for Clark County. Please help me explain how we can leverage data analytics for better planning and decision-making.

350. I am the Transparency Coordinator for King County. Please help me discuss methods for ensuring transparency during the strategic planning process.

351. I am the Strategy Assessment Director for Johnson County. Please help me plan how to assess and adapt our strategic plan on a regular basis.

352. As a county manager, describe a plan to approach balancing the needs of urban and rural areas in the strategic plan.

353. I am a Small Business Advocate working in Willowbrook. Please help me support local entrepreneurs and businesses by creating programs that boost economic growth and entrepreneurship.

354. Imagine you're the Social Media Manager for Augusta. Discuss how you would leverage social media platforms to enhance public engagement and disseminate information effectively.

355. You're the Video Production Coordinator in Roswell. Discuss how you would create compelling video content to educate and engage the public.

TECHNOLOGY & INNOVATION

356. I am going to give you a writing sample that I want you to learn my voice, for future prompt responses.

357. Write a cover letter for an application to the ___ City Manager position. I want to highlight my experience as a ___, my work in ___, as well as my current role as the ___ in ___. Tailor the cover letter to the job ad given below:

358. write a city code that addresses barking dogs

359. Give me 5 things I can use ChatGPT for as a city manager

360. As a city manager what are some grants to launch a behavioral health crisis response team in my city?

361. prepare a template for submitting progress report to CDBG program administrators and other relevant stakeholders

362. I am the deputy city manager, and I am drafting a report to the city manager on the topic of addressing oversized trucks on city streets. Here are the meeting notes. Please help me craft a memo based on this information.

363. I am a city manager in ___ and im interested in this grant. Please tell me the grant requirements and help me understand the staff time and other costs that may be associated with the grant.

364. This is the link to the Maricopa City Code; I want to create PDFs of each section that I can download

365. please create a bar chart of vehicle license tax (VLT) revenues

by city based on this data. use differentiating colors for each city.

366. i am the city manager of loss altos' hills ca. i want to evaluate this request for ___: [insert request]. Please recommend ways for me to do that. What questions should I ask? and what data should I request to better justify or reject the request?

367. I have three job descriptions im going to upload. PLEASE WAIT

368. the following is a chart of state shared revenues for cities and towns in arizona. I want you to recommend 3 ways to visualize this data.

369. explain in one paragraph what happens when a car's wheels are not aligned. Then use that example to talk about misalignment in a city.

370. Give me 5 ideas for a text to video. I want the video to be something related to city government.

371. I will give you a question or an instruction. Your objective is to answer my question or follow my instruction. My question or instruction is search for any studies on ambulance interfacility transport.

372. Write me VBA code for a PowerPoint presentation on the permitting process for the city of ___. Fill in all the text with information from: [link to permitting information]. No placeholders. I need 5 slides.

373. summarize this strategic plan for Gila County, AZ. take that summary and use it to write the VBA for a 7-slide presentation.

374. Learn and summarize this strategic plan. Then suggest new goals that are in line with and build from the current goals. Turn the new goals into a presentation.

375. I have a document I want to get insights on. For context, we are approaching this conversation as leaders in the city of ___. All responses must keep that in mind and must be in the best interest of the city of ___.

376. give me some alternate job titles for Senior Advisor

377. find research papers on the most efficient ways to transport humans and goods for cities

378. reword the following for clarity and conciseness

379. help me create some activities to foster discussion on work alignment to the city objectives and mission

380. You are a hiring manager for the city. Your job is to evaluate 3 resumes against a job description to find the best candidate. We are prioritizing leadership experience. Here are the resumes: [insert resumes] And here's the job description [insert job description]

381. [upload public sector workforce data from the US Census Bureau] now what if i am a city manager in alaska. what insights can a get from this dataset?

382. [upload public sector workforce data from the US Census Bureau] give me 5 ways to do a statewide comparison analysis using this dataset as the city manager of Seward AK

383. you are the city manager of murray utah. you need to understand the liabilities, 2nd and 3rd order effects of this request:

384. This is a dataset of rentals with the mailing address being the property owner's address and the site address being the address of the rental property. I want to know how many have a mailing address that is non-local. We are defining non-local addresses as a mailing address with a PO Box or a city that is not North Bend or Coos Bay.

385. I am a communications director for a city in Oregon. What can I learn from this social media page [insert link] to help me with my city's social media presence?

386. Please recommend some analysis from this data. For context, I am a City Manager in Wisconsin

387. Please do a municipality comparison for Stevens Point, WI and Whitewater, WI

388. Please use these files to do a historical trend analysis of state-shared revenues for the City of Milton, WI

389. Please write the VBA code for me to put this presentation into PowerPoint.

390. I am going to be giving a presentation on ___ at ___. Please give me 10 catchy titles for my session. My focus is on ____ and the audience is primarily ____.

391. Please convert this to a spreadsheet with the following as headers:

392. I am evaluating the need and function of ___ position. Attached is a compilation of essential duties from various ____ job descriptions across the country. First i want you to use this to create a list of unique duties in bulleted format.

393. Now I want to summarize this whole conversation into a white paper. make this a 3–5-page paper. also include some of the 2nd and 3rd order effects

394. Make this sound better and help it flow more cohesively

395. please help me rewrite the following draft email for clarity, conciseness, and professionalism. I want to make it a friendly and positive tone, while also giving clear directions to staff.

396. I am an Animal Shelter Manager for the County of ___. Propose an initiative to improve animal adoption rates from shelters.

397. I am an Animal Control Officer in the city of ___. How can we better control stray animal populations?

398. I am the city manager of ___ Describe how data analytics could help in municipal decision-making.

399. I am a planner for the city of ____. Propose a long-term urban planning initiative.

400. I am a city manager in ____. How can we improve the response time for public queries and complaints?

401. I am a streets manager for the city of ___. Propose a bicycle-friendly initiative.

402. You are a public transit manager for the city of ____. Suggest ways to expand or improve public transit routes.

403. I am a business analyst for the city of ____. Suggest a plan to improve financial accountability.

404. I am the HR Manager for the city of ____. How can we improve onboarding for new hires?

405. I am the HR Director for the city of ___. Propose a mentorship program within the municipality.

406. I am a public information officer for the city of ___. Suggest a newsletter to keep residents informed of municipal activities.

407. I am the city manager for ____. Describe how to establish a municipal podcast.

408. I am the IT director for the city of ___. How can we improve the municipal website's user experience [insert link to website]?

409. I am the Assistant City Manager in ____. How can we make local government processes more transparent?

410. I am a CIP manager for the city of ___. Create an asset replacement plan.

411. List three initiatives for improving the municipality's public image.

412. I am a permit technician for the city of ___. Describe a strategy to streamline permit applications.

413. I am the facilities manager for the city of ___. How can we extend the lifespan of our municipal buildings?

414. I am a garbage collection driver for the city of___. Describe a system for more efficient garbage collection routes.

415. Describe a plan to deal with water main breaks and leaks.

416. I am a fleet manager for the city of ___. Suggest a system for tracking the utilization of municipal vehicles.

417. Describe how to conduct a fleet efficiency audit.

418. I am a grants analyst for the city of ___. Suggest ways to secure grants or partnerships for special projects.

419. Efficient communication is the lifeblood of a successful department. How can we streamline communication processes within our department to ensure information flows seamlessly and timely among team members?

420. Imagine you're the Traffic Signal Optimization Planner in Oceanview Harbor. Share your detailed plan for improving traffic signal coordination throughout our city.

421. Assume the role of Event Crowd Control Supervisor in Forest Brook and describe innovative strategies and techniques for maintaining effective crowd control during public events in our city.

422. Suggest ways to prioritize asset repair and replacement.

423. Assume the position of Financial Reporting and Transparency Officer in Willowbrook Springs and discuss the best practices to enhance financial reporting and transparency within the municipality.

424. Assume the position of Financial Forecasting Expert in Riverwood Hills. Share the best practices that can be adopted to improve the accuracy of our financial forecasting.

425. How can the municipality take advantage of bulk purchasing?

426. Describe a strategy for reducing long-term financial liabilities.

427. Propose a plan for preparing for external financial audits.

428. As the Internal Controls Enhancement Manager in Silverwood Heights, outline strategies to improve internal controls, ensuring successful financial audits for the municipality.

429. Assume the position of Investment Portfolio Manager in Cedarbrook Falls and discuss the best strategy for managing the municipality's investment portfolio.

430. Assume the position of Tax Collection Efficiency Director in Forest Ridge. Describe how to make the tax collection process more efficient, optimizing revenue for the municipality.

431. You're the Tax Delinquency Reduction Manager in Meadowbrook Springs. Propose methods to reduce tax delinquency rates within our municipality.

432. In your role as the Fee Collection Modernization Expert in Riverwood Pines, suggest innovative approaches to modernize and streamline fee collection for our municipality.

433. As the Revenue Diversification Planner in Maplewood Bluffs, propose alternative revenue-generating initiatives like tourism promotion or special business zones.

434. Describe a framework for evaluating the ROI on capital investments.

435. Describe criteria for selecting private partners for municipal projects.

436. What are some long-term benefits of investing in sustainability?

437. What are some key financial performance indicators that should be monitored?

438. Describe a system for real-time monitoring of financial KPIs.

439. Suggest methods for benchmarking our financial performance against other municipalities.

440. Suggest criteria for evaluating the performance of

contractors and suppliers.

441. How can we ensure that contract terms are aligned with municipal objectives?

442. I am working on ensuring equitable pay across departments in Columbia, Missouri. What strategies can we use to achieve fair and consistent pay practices?

443. I am working on promoting diversity and inclusion in hiring and promotions in Burnsville, Minnesota. What strategies can we implement to foster diversity and inclusion throughout HR processes?

444. I am working on a strategy for succession planning in key roles in Maple Grove, Minnesota. How can we ensure a smooth transition in key positions within the organization?

445. How can we ensure confidentiality in HR processes?

446. Describe an approach for periodic HR audits.

447. What are some criteria for deciding between internal promotions and external hires?

448. How can we improve our methods for skills assessment during recruitment?

449. How can we facilitate better teamwork across departments?

450. I am working on managing layoffs or restructuring to minimize negative impact in St. Cloud, Minnesota. What considerations and practices can be employed to handle these situations with care and compassion?

451. I am working on an approach for ethical decision-making in HR in Owasso, Oklahoma. How can we ensure that HR decisions are made ethically and align with the organization's values?

452. I am working on promoting a culture of continuous improvement in Blue Springs, Missouri. What initiatives and practices can foster a culture of ongoing enhancement within the organization?

453. I am working on how HR can support the organization's strategic goals in Minnetonka, Minnesota. What role can HR play in aligning HR practices with the strategic objectives of the organization?

454. I am working on making the hiring process more efficient in St. Joseph, Missouri. What steps and tools can be implemented to streamline and expedite the hiring process?

455. I am working on HR's contribution to innovation within the organization in Galveston, Texas. How can HR foster innovation?

456. I am working on managing outsourcing and its impact on internal staff in Frisco, Texas. How can we effectively handle this impact?

457. I am working on work-life balance initiatives in Palm Bay, Florida. What strategies should we adopt to promote work-life balance?

458. I am working on a model for peer reviews within the organization in Pensacola, Florida. Can you suggest an effective model for peer reviews?

459. I am working on creative recruitment advertising strategies in Odessa, Texas. What creative methods can we use for recruitment?

460. I am working on conducting exit interviews to glean insights in Brownsville, Texas. What process should we follow for these interviews?

461. I am working on creating a more inclusive environment for people with disabilities in Beaumont, Texas. How can we achieve this inclusivity?

462. I am working on effective team-building activities in College Station, Texas. What methods can we use for successful team building?

463. I am working on methods for fostering a culture of creativity in Port St. Lucie, Florida. How can we promote a creative culture

within the organization?

464. I am working on addressing gender disparities in pay and opportunities in Rio Rancho. How can we effectively address these disparities?

465. I am working on measures to ensure equal opportunities for part-time workers in Hobbs. What measures should we consider?

466. I am working on integrating sustainability goals into HR practices in Gallup. How can we better integrate sustainability goals into HR?

467. I am working on assessing HR initiatives in Dover. What are effective ways to evaluate the impact of HR initiatives on organizational performance?

468. I am working on HR policies for workplace harassment and discrimination in Newark. What are some important guidelines for dealing with workplace harassment and discrimination?

469. I am working on organizational growth strategies in Wilmington. How can we effectively manage the challenges that come with rapid organizational growth?

470. I am working on HR strategies for organizational sustainability in Cleveland. How can HR contribute to achieving long-term organizational sustainability?

471. I am working on active shooter preparedness in New York City. Could you describe a comprehensive plan for active shooter preparedness that we can implement?

472. I am working on measures to combat drug-related crime in Syracuse. What measures and strategies can be employed to effectively combat drug-related crime in our city?

473. I am a Privacy and Surveillance Expert working in Harmonyville. Please help me describe methods for improving surveillance without compromising privacy.

474. I am a Technology Integration Specialist working in

Greenfield. Please help me make better use of technology in disaster response.

475. I am working on biohazard threat response for Richland County, SC. Please help me describe a plan for dealing with biohazard threats.

476. I am working on Business Attraction for Eau Claire County, WI. Please help me identify ways to attract new businesses to Eau Claire County, such as offering incentives, improving the business environment, and promoting economic opportunities.

477. I am working on Historic Preservation for Ozaukee County, WI. Please help me describe a strategy for historic preservation in Ozaukee County, including the identification and protection of historically significant sites and buildings.

478. I am working on Public Transportation Enhancement for Williamson County, TN. Please help me identify strategies for enhancing public transportation options in Williamson County, including expanding routes, improving accessibility, and promoting ridership.

479. I am working on business attraction for Maricopa County. Please help me identify ways to attract new businesses to Maricopa County, such as offering incentives, improving the business environment, and promoting economic opportunities.

480. I am working on historic preservation for Charleston County. Please help me describe a strategy for historic preservation in Charleston County, including the identification and protection of historically significant sites and buildings.

481. I am working on public transportation enhancement for Cook County. Please help me identify strategies for enhancing public transportation options in Cook County, including expanding routes, improving accessibility, and promoting ridership.

482. I am working on urban design for the city of Gaithersburg.

Please help me consider considerations for pedestrian-friendly urban design, including walkability assessments, safe crossing designs, green space integration, and streetscape enhancements.

483. I am working on environmental impact assessment for the city of Salisbury. Please help me describe methods for assessing the environmental impact of new projects, considering factors like sustainability, ecological conservation, and mitigation strategies.

484. I am a City Planner working on improving residential street design for the city of Sioux Falls. Please help me explore ways to enhance street layouts, sidewalks, bike lanes, and traffic calming measures to create safer and more user-friendly residential streets.

485. I am a Transportation Planner working on facilitating environmentally friendly transportation options like bike lanes and walking paths for the city of Champaign. Please help me outline methods for integrating these options into urban planning, promoting sustainable mobility, and reducing car dependency.

486. I am an Energy Analyst working on improving the energy efficiency of public buildings for the city of Flagstaff. Please help me describe initiatives such as energy audits, renewable energy installations, and green building standards to reduce energy consumption.

487. I am a Streetscape Designer working on enhancing streetscapes and public pathways for the city of Avondale. Please help me discuss beautification efforts, pedestrian-friendly design, and public art installations to create inviting public spaces.

488. I am working on increasing green spaces in urban areas for the city of Chattanooga. Please help me describe a plan that includes the conversion of unused spaces, vertical gardens, and green rooftops to enhance greenery and improve urban environments.

489. I am working on educational programming in nature reserves for the city of Kalamazoo. Please help me identify opportunities for educational programming within our nature reserves, such as guided hikes, wildlife observation, and interactive workshops to promote environmental awareness.

490. In Cedar Rapids, we optimize the use of open spaces for both organized events and leisurely activities by developing multi-purpose areas with flexible layouts, allowing for a wide range of activities from sports events to picnics and relaxation.

491. In Sioux City, we combat soil erosion in hiking areas by implementing erosion control measures such as planting native vegetation, installing retaining walls, and maintaining well-defined trails to prevent soil erosion and protect natural habitats.

492. In Racine, we incorporate innovative playground features that cater to various skills and interests, such as inclusive play structures, nature-based play areas, and sensory-rich elements that engage children of all abilities.

493. In Bellevue, we are improving picnic areas by adding shaded pavilions, upgrading seating and tables, and providing better waste disposal facilities to enhance the overall picnic experience for our residents.

494. In Grand Island, we facilitate birdwatching and wildlife observation activities by creating dedicated viewing areas, offering guided tours, and providing educational materials to help visitors appreciate and respect the local fauna.

495. In Norfolk, we optimize scheduling to maximize the use of sports fields and courts by implementing online reservation systems and coordinating with local sports organizations to ensure efficient and fair access to these facilities.

496. I am the Business Attraction Strategist for the city of Rehoboth Beach. Please help me describe our strategy for attracting new businesses to our city, fostering economic growth and job creation.

497. I am the Small Business Support Coordinator for the city of Helena. Please help me discuss how local government can provide support to existing small businesses, helping them thrive and grow.

498. I am the Green Initiatives Incentives Manager for the city of Olympia. Please help me explore incentives that can be offered to companies for embracing green initiatives, contributing to environmental sustainability and economic growth.

499. I am the International Trade and Investment Advisor for the city of Providence. Please help me describe our approach to international trade and investment, expanding our city's economic reach and global opportunities.

500. I am the Talent Retention Strategist for the city of Aurora. Please help me outline strategies to retain talent in our city, ensuring we keep our skilled workforce engaged and contributing to our local economy.

501. I am the Downtown Revitalization Planner for the city of Eugene. Please help me identify strategies to make our downtown area more vibrant and attractive for residents and businesses.

502. I am the Data Analytics Specialist for Economic Planning for the city of Spokane. Please help me elaborate on how data analytics can be effectively utilized in economic planning and decision-making processes.

503. I am the Historical Site Economic Utilization Coordinator for the city of Santa Barbara. Please help me describe how historical sites can be leveraged for economic benefit, preserving our heritage while contributing to our local economy.

504. I am the Business Incubator Program Manager for the city of Portland. Please help me outline a comprehensive plan for establishing a business incubator that nurtures and supports startups and entrepreneurs in our mid-sized city.

505. I am the Regional Collaboration Liaison for the city of Salt

Lake City. Please help me explore strategies for collaboration with neighboring regions to promote mutual economic growth and prosperity.

506. I am the Tax Incentives Evaluation Manager for the city of Louisville. Please help me analyze the advantages and disadvantages of offering tax breaks to large corporations and their potential impact on our local economy.

507. My work focuses on liaising with nonprofit partners in the city of Fresno. Please help me elaborate on the vital role nonprofits play in fostering a healthy and resilient local economy.

508. I am the Tourism Marketing Manager for the city of Omaha. Please help me describe a comprehensive tourism marketing campaign aimed at attracting visitors and boosting our local economy.

509. I am the International Trade Relations Coordinator for the city of Spokane. Please help me explore strategies to improve trade relations with other cities or countries, bolstering our local economy.

510. I am the Elderly Population Support Advocate for the city of Boise. Please help me discuss how we can better support the elderly population's participation in the economy, considering their unique needs and contributions to our mid-sized city.

511. I am the Smart City Initiative Coordinator for the city of Knoxville. Please help me describe a "smart city" initiative tailored to our mid-sized city that can significantly boost economic growth through technology and data-driven solutions.

512. I am the Festivals and Public Events Economic Analyst for the city of Little Rock. Please help me assess and quantify the economic impact of festivals and public events in our mid-sized city.

513. I am the Local Fashion and Design Industry Liaison for the city of Sacramento. Please help me identify strategies to support

and nurture the growth of our local fashion and design industries.

514. I am the Apprenticeship and Internship Coordinator for the city of Tulsa. Please help me explore ways to incentivize and encourage businesses to offer apprenticeships and internships, benefiting both our local workforce and economy.

515. I am the Public Art and Beautification Projects Manager for the city of Birmingham. Please help me discuss the positive impact of public art and beautification projects on local businesses and their role in enhancing our city's appeal.

516. I am the Child Care Affordability Advocate for the city of Omaha. Please help me elaborate on how affordable childcare can have a positive impact on our local economy and workforce.

517. I am the Business Cost Reduction Director for the city of Albuquerque. Please help me discuss the initiatives we can implement to reduce the cost of doing business in our city, fostering economic growth.

518. I am the Consumer Affairs Director for the city of Phoenix. Please help me explore strategies to encourage consumer spending and boost our local economy.

519. I am the Quality-of-Life Analyst for the city of Denver. Please help me identify methods to measure and enhance the quality of life as a crucial economic indicator for our city.

520. I am the Small Business Mentorship Program Manager for the city of Boston. Please help me discuss the benefits and implementation of a mentorship program designed to support and empower local businesses.

521. I am the Branding and Identity Manager for the city of San Jose. Please help me describe the steps and strategies to create a unique city brand and identity that resonates with residents and visitors alike.

522. I am the Business Ethics Coordinator for the city of Houston. Please help me elucidate methods to promote ethical business

practices among our local companies.

523. I am the Small Business Networking Coordinator for the city of New York. Please help me develop a plan to facilitate networking opportunities for local businesses and foster collaboration.

524. I am the Talent Attraction Manager for the city of Seattle. Please help me devise methods to attract high-skilled labor to our city to bolster our economy.

525. I am the Night-Time Economy Coordinator for the city of Las Vegas. Please help me outline strategies for developing and sustaining a vibrant night-time economy.

526. I am the Veterans Workforce Director for the city of San Diego. Please help me discuss how we can best support veterans in re-entering the workforce and leveraging their skills.

527. I am the Sustainable Agriculture Director for the city of Portland. Please help me discuss some innovative strategies for encouraging sustainable fisheries or farming practices.

528. I am the Circular Economy Coordinator for the city of Boston. Please help me explain how a circular economy can be encouraged at the municipal level to reduce waste and improve sustainability.

529. I am the Workforce Mental Health Director for the city of Denver. Please help me outline ways to support mental health as a critical factor in workforce productivity.

530. I am the Indigenous Relations Officer for the city of Albuquerque. Please help me describe our approach to managing economic relations with indigenous communities respectfully and beneficially.

531. I am the Business Chamber Liaison for the city of Dallas. Please help me explain how we can foster stronger relationships with local business chambers and associations to spur economic growth.

532. I am the Retail Diversity Coordinator for the city of New York.

Please help me describe some strategies for promoting a diverse range of retail options to enrich our local economy.

533. What initiatives can be put in place to promote reading among teenagers?

534. How can you develop programs that reflect cultural heritage and diversity?

535. Describe a system for public feedback and how it could be used for continuous improvement.

536. How can libraries adapt to technological changes without losing their traditional essence?

537. Discuss ways to encourage literacy and a love for reading in adults.

538. Describe the process for creating a unified strategic vision for the city or county.

539. What methods can be used to align departmental goals with the overall strategic plan?

540. Describe the role of public input in shaping city or county goals.

541. Discuss methods for monitoring the implementation of strategic initiatives.

542. I am the Adaptability Consultant for Hamilton County. Please help me discuss the importance of adaptability in the county's strategic plan.

543. I am the Prioritization Analyst for Lincoln County. Please help me explore how to manage competing priorities between different county departments.

544. I am the Environmental Planning Manager for Wayne County. Please help me discuss ways to incorporate sustainability and environmental goals into our strategic planning.

545. How can you build and maintain relationships with state and

federal government for collaborative projects?

546. I am the Innovation Director for the city of Austin. Please help me articulate what role innovation plays in our city's strategic planning efforts.

547. I am the Legacy Planning Coordinator for the city of Miami. Please help me discuss the importance of legacy and how our current plans will affect future generations.

548. I am the Public-Private Partnerships Manager for the city of Minneapolis. Please help me explore how public-private partnerships can be used to achieve our strategic objectives.

549. I am the Ethics Officer for the city of Philadelphia. Please help me describe ways to ensure that ethical considerations are seamlessly integrated into our strategic planning.

550. I am the Accountability Manager for the city of Baltimore. Please help me outline how we can ensure accountability in executing our strategic plan.

551. I am the Social Impact Analyst for the city of Milwaukee. Please help me discuss methods for evaluating the social impact of our strategic initiatives.

552. I am the Smart City Coordinator for the city of Raleigh. Please help me elucidate what role smart city technologies will play in our strategic planning.

553. I am the Public Health Director for the city of Sacramento. Please help me describe ways to incorporate health and well-being objectives into our strategic plan.

554. I am the Planning Analyst for the city of Indianapolis. Please help me identify what tools can be used for scenario planning and forecasting in our strategic planning efforts.

555. How can you prepare for leadership transitions without disrupting strategic objectives?

556. I am the Chief Strategy Officer for the city of Boston. Please

help me describe methods for resolving conflicts that arise during strategic planning and execution to ensure successful outcomes.

557. I am the Economic Advisor for the city of Seattle. Please help me design a strategic plan that is resilient to economic fluctuations to maintain stability and growth.

558. I am the Director of Transportation for the city of Atlanta. Please help me discuss strategies for enhancing public transportation as part of our city's goals to improve mobility and reduce congestion.

559. How can a focus on mental health be integrated into city or county objectives?

560. I am a Senior HR Analyst, and I am creating a job description for _____ position. Please help me review, edit and add KSA for this job description. I want the KSAs to line up with the essential duties and responsibilities. This is what I have so far: [Paste job description text]

561. I am a Sustainability Officer working in Greenfield. Please help me create initiatives to make our city eco-friendlier, reduce its carbon footprint, and promote sustainable practices.

562. I am a Youth Program Manager working in Sunville. Please help me design engaging and educational programs for our youth, including after-school activities and workshops.

563. I am a Cultural Events Coordinator working in Harmonyville. Please help me organize cultural festivals, art exhibitions, and performances that celebrate our city's diversity and heritage.

564. You're the Transit Accessibility Coordinator based in Montgomery. Discuss methods to enhance accessibility for passengers with disabilities within our transit system.

565. In your role as the Transit Fare Integration Specialist in Auburn, outline a strategy for streamlining fare payment systems across various modes of public transportation.

566. As the Transit Customer Experience Analyst in Hoover,

describe how to gather and analyze feedback to improve the overall transit experience for passengers.

567. You're the Transit Sustainability Coordinator in Decatur. Propose initiatives and policies to make our transit system more environmentally sustainable.

568. As the Public Information Officer in Atlanta, outline a crisis communication plan for responding to major incidents or disasters within the city.

569. Assume the position of Graphic Designer in Athens. Describe how you would create visually appealing and informative materials for public campaigns.

570. In your role as the Web Content Manager for Columbus, propose improvements to the city's website to make information more accessible to residents.

571. Assume the position of Public Information Assistant in Johns Creek. Describe your role in supporting the Public Information Officer and handling various communication tasks for the city.

572. In your role as the Claims Adjuster in Wilmington, describe your approach to managing and processing claims efficiently while minimizing financial losses for the city.

PUBLIC ENGAGEMENT

573. I am the community director for lake park florida and i want to create a community survey on youth recreation leagues. Please draft a survey that will go out to parents of children between the ages of 8-15 and are in the city's youth recreational league.

574. Find me 5 grants I can apply for to do road repairs in my community.

575. Give me 5 grants for community engagement that a city should consider exploring.

576. I am the Parks and Recreation Director for the City ____. I want to create a community survey on youth sports recreation leagues.

577. give me examples of forms that cities might use for community engagement.

578. This is a draft city budget for the town of Oceanside florida. I need help taking this information and making it more accessible and understandable to the community. Recommend ways to do that.

579. Write the vba code for a 15 slide powerpoint presentation on work alignment with mission objectives for supervisors in the City of Maricopa. The city mission is to Unlock the full potential of the City of Maricopa to create a thriving and durable community. The city's objectives are 1. Maintain and enhance Maricopa's physical environment; 2. Ensure a safe and durable community; 3. Promote economic vitality and sustainable community; 4. Be a premier city.

580. I am an Animal Control Officer in the city of ___. Suggest community education programs about responsible pet ownership.

581. I am a development services director for the city of ___. Suggest ways to utilize GIS mapping for community improvement.

582. I am a community services director for the city of ___. How can we promote and preserve local history?

583. I am a community services director for the city of ___. Describe how to maintain or update public art installations.

584. I am a communications director for the city of ___. Propose a social media strategy to improve community engagement.

585. I am a community services manager for the city of ___. Propose an event series to foster community engagement.

586. I am a community services director for the city of ___. How can we make our community centers more inclusive?

587. I am the recycling manager for the city of ___. Propose a comprehensive recycling program for the community.

588. What are some alternative funding mechanisms like municipal bonds or community fundraising?

589. I am working on community outreach and public relations for HR in Las Cruces. What role does HR play in community outreach and public relations?

590. I am working on improving community policing initiatives in Akron. Could you describe a comprehensive plan for enhancing community policing efforts?

591. Describe methods for combating the opioid crisis at a community level in Toledo.

592. How can we foster a culture of safety within the community in Toledo?

593. I am a Community Safety Advisor working in Greenfield. Please help me discuss the role citizens play in ensuring their own safety.

594. I am a Disaster Recovery Planner working in Harmonyville. Please help me explore how we can ensure effective disaster recovery and community resilience.

595. I am a Diversity and Inclusion Officer working in Hillside. Please help me explore how public safety can be tailored to meet the needs of a diverse community.

596. I am a Senior Safety Specialist working in Meadowbrook. Please help me explore how we can improve the safety of senior citizens in the community.

597. I am working on community-based solutions to crime prevention for Utah County, UT. Please help me suggest a program for community-based solutions to crime prevention.

598. I am working on Public Art Integration for La Crosse County, WI. Please help me explore ways to integrate public art into community development in La Crosse County, enhancing the cultural and aesthetic aspects of the region.

599. I am working on Waterfront Development for Door County, WI. Please help me outline a plan for developing waterfront areas in Door County, including recreational amenities, environmental considerations, and community engagement.

600. I am working on Community Engagement in Zoning for Santa Cruz County, AZ. Please help me describe methods for involving the community in zoning decisions in Santa Cruz County, ensuring transparency, and fostering public participation.

601. I am working on Gentrification Solutions for Haywood County, TN. Please help me discuss how we can address gentrification issues in Haywood County, including affordable housing strategies, equitable development, and community

preservation.

602. I am working on public art integration for Los Angeles County. Please help me explore ways to integrate public art into community development in Los Angeles County, enhancing the cultural and aesthetic aspects of the region.

603. I am working on waterfront development for King County. Please help me outline a plan for developing waterfront areas in King County, including recreational amenities, environmental considerations, and community engagement.

604. I am working on community engagement in zoning for Santa Clara County. Please help me describe methods for involving the community in zoning decisions in Santa Clara County, ensuring transparency, and fostering public participation.

605. I am working on gentrification solutions for Fulton County. Please help me discuss how we can address gentrification issues in Fulton County, including affordable housing strategies, equitable development, and community preservation.

606. I am working on rural development initiatives for the city of Hagerstown. Please help me identify ways to encourage development in rural or underserved areas, such as providing economic incentives, upgrading infrastructure, and engaging the local community.

607. I am a Senior Services Coordinator working on facilitating elderly-friendly development for the city of Rapid City. Please help me outline strategies like age-inclusive housing, accessible infrastructure, and senior-oriented services to support elderly residents in our community.

608. I am a Community Engagement Specialist working on promoting the use of public spaces in Brookings. Please help me outline methods such as community events, recreational programs, and beautification efforts that encourage residents to utilize and enjoy public spaces.

609. I am a facilities Manager working on improving community facilities like libraries, pools, and sports centers in Vermillion. Please help me discuss renovation plans, accessibility upgrades, and programming initiatives that enhance the functionality and appeal of these facilities.

610. I am a Community Planner working on ensuring that new developments are well-integrated into the existing community for the city of Elgin. Please help me explore strategies such as mixed-use zoning, neighborhood engagement, and infrastructure connections to create seamless transitions between new and existing areas.

611. I am a Redevelopment Manager working on a strategy for revitalizing disused public spaces in Springfield. Please help me outline plans for repurposing vacant lots, underutilized parks, or abandoned buildings to revitalize public spaces and enhance community use.

612. I am a Community Organizer working on fostering community cohesiveness through development for the city of Peoria. Please help me discuss strategies like community events, neighborhood associations, and inclusive planning processes that promote unity and collaboration among residents.

613. I am a Youth Engagement Coordinator working on involving youth in community development initiatives for the city of Bloomington. Please help me identify strategies such as youth advisory councils, mentorship programs, and youth-led projects that engage young residents in shaping their community.

614. I am a Community Development Planner working on creating more co-working and community office spaces for the city of Bolingbrook. Please help me outline plans for shared workspaces, incubator hubs, and flexible office solutions that foster entrepreneurship and collaboration.

615. I am a Cultural Affairs Manager working on supporting local arts and culture through development for the city of Cicero. Please

help me explore ways to integrate public art, cultural institutions, and artist spaces into new developments, enriching the cultural fabric of the community.

616. I am a Community Planner working on enhancing resident well-being in high-density housing for the city of Mesa. Please help me describe methods like green spaces, community centers, and wellness programs that can improve the quality of life for residents in high-density housing.

617. I am an Economic Development Specialist working on encouraging local food production through urban farming for the city of Gilbert. Please help me identify methods such as community gardens, rooftop farms, and agricultural initiatives that support urban farming practices.

618. I am a Housing Planner working on fostering inclusivity in new housing developments for the city of Surprise. Please help me outline measures such as affordable housing options, accessible design, and community engagement to create inclusive housing communities.

619. I am an Economic Development Manager working on encouraging developers to invest in our community for the city of Goodyear. Please help me outline incentives, partnerships, and infrastructure improvements that can attract and retain developers in our city.

620. I am a Development Services Analyst working on regularly updating and revising development codes and guidelines for the city of Maricopa. Please help me outline a process for staying current with emerging best practices, incorporating community feedback, and maintaining a responsive regulatory framework.

621. I am working on initiatives to promote outdoor activity and wellness in Franklin. Please help me outline programs like fitness classes, walking trails, and wellness campaigns that encourage healthy lifestyles among our community members.

622. I am working on engaging the community in park

management and conservation efforts in Johnson City. Please help me explore methods such as volunteer programs, citizen science projects, and community-led initiatives to involve residents in caring for our parks.

623. I am working on a plan for a community garden and its potential benefits in Murfreesboro. Please help me outline the design, gardening plots, educational programs, and community-building opportunities that a community garden can offer.

624. I am working on introducing programming to promote cultural diversity in South Bend's parks. Please help me describe the types of events, festivals, and educational programs that can celebrate cultural diversity and foster inclusivity within our community.

625. I am working on combating vandalism and maintaining park aesthetics in Fishers. Please help me explore effective strategies such as surveillance, community involvement, and graffiti removal initiatives to preserve the beauty of our parks.

626. I am working on using parks to enhance community cohesiveness in Bloomington. Please help me outline strategies like community gardening, group fitness classes, and cultural events that bring residents together and strengthen social bonds.

627. I am working on encouraging local businesses to sponsor parks and recreational activities in Lafayette. Please help me explore incentives and promotional opportunities for businesses to support and engage with our community through park sponsorship.

628. In West Des Moines, we identify community partnership opportunities for enhancing recreational services by collaborating with local non-profits, schools, businesses, and community groups to offer additional programs, events, and amenities in our parks, enriching the recreational experiences available to our residents.

629. In La Crosse, we describe a plan for a skate park,

including design, safety measures, and community involvement. We engage local skateboarders, solicit input from the community, and collaborate with professional designers to create a safe and appealing skate park that meets the needs of our residents.

630. In Fremont, we are developing an adventure and obstacle course within a park to promote active and challenging recreational opportunities, attracting thrill-seekers and fitness enthusiasts from the community.

631. I am working on accessibility and inclusivity for the city of Jonesboro's Parks and Recreation Department. Please help me describe methods for creating sensory gardens within our parks, catering to the needs and experiences of the visually impaired community.

632. I am working on community engagement for the city of Bentonville's Parks and Recreation Department. Please help me describe a strategy for implementing a successful farmers market in a park setting, promoting local produce and community interaction.

633. I am working on citizen science initiatives for the city of Fort Smith's Parks and Recreation Department. Please help me explore ways to foster community science projects within our parks, encouraging scientific exploration and learning.

634. I am the Social Media Promotion Coordinator for the city of Austin's Parks and Recreation Department. Please help me outline a plan for promoting park programs and activities effectively through social media, engaging our community and attracting participants.

635. I am working on senior engagement for the city of San Diego's Parks and Recreation Department. Please help me identify methods for involving elderly community members in park activities, promoting their active participation and well-being.

636. I am the Community Mural Project Manager for the city of Asheville and the Recreation Department. Please help me outline

a strategy for a community mural project within one of our parks, engaging local artists and residents in a collaborative endeavor.

637. I am the Park's Communication Coordinator for the city of Tempe. Please help me identify methods to regularly update the community on park developments and changes, ensuring transparency and community involvement.

638. I am the Amphitheater Development Coordinator for the city of Champaign. Please help me outline a plan for an amphitheater designed for community events and performances, providing a cultural and entertainment hub for our residents.

639. I am the Recreational Equipment Rentals Manager for the city of San Diego. Please help me explore ways to offer rentals of recreational equipment like paddle boats or bicycles in our parks, providing additional recreational opportunities for our community.

640. I am the Community Outreach and Social Programs Coordinator for the city of Buffalo. Please help me identify ways to use parks as venues for community outreach and social programs, fostering community engagement and well-being in our urban spaces.

641. I am the Community Well-being Assessment Manager for the city of Cornwalis. Please help me explore how we can measure the impact of parks and recreational activities on community well-being in our unique urban environment.

642. I am the Tourism and Economic Development Director for the city of Concord. Please help me discuss the role of tourism in economic development and how we can leverage our attractions to benefit our community.

643. I am the Affordable Housing Accessibility Planner for the city of Greenville. Please help me discuss strategies for improving access to affordable housing in relation to economic development, ensuring everyone in our community can thrive.

644. I am the Industrial Area Revitalization Planner for the city of Burlington. Please help me describe a plan for revitalizing a declining industrial area, bringing new life and economic opportunities to the community.

645. I am the Entrepreneurship Promotion Specialist for the city of Olympia. Please help me explore ways to encourage entrepreneurship within our community, fostering innovation and job creation.

646. I am the Inclusivity and Economic Development Coordinator for the city of Santa Barbara. Please help me outline our approach to ensuring that the economic plan is inclusive and benefits all community members, promoting equity and social well-being alongside economic growth.

647. I am the Arts and Culture Development Coordinator for the city of Santa Fe. Please help me discuss how arts and culture contribute to economic development in our culturally rich community.

648. I am the Public Transport Economic Integration Manager for the city of Anchorage. Please help me explore how public transport can be leveraged to generate economic gains and improve accessibility within our community.

649. I am the Minority-Owned Business Promotion Director for the city of Providence. Please help me outline a plan to promote and support minority-owned businesses within our community.

650. I am the "Shop Local" Campaign Coordinator for the city of Austin. Please help me elucidate how our city can benefit from a "Shop Local" campaign, stimulating economic growth and community support.

651. I am the Young Professionals Attraction Strategist for the city of Denver. Please help me identify methods to attract and retain young professionals in our community, enhancing our city's talent pool and innovation.

652. I am the Economic Resilience Coordinator for the city of Columbus. Please help me discuss strategies for crisis recovery and building economic resilience within our community.

653. I am a project manager focusing on renewable energy for the city of Tucson. Please help me describe a plan for a large-scale renewable energy project that can benefit our community's economy and sustainability.

654. My work for the City of Oklahoma City focuses on industry revitalization. Please help me explore ways to support industries facing economic decline in our community, aiming to revitalize and transform them for sustained growth.

655. I work in Business Development for the city of Kansas City. Please help me outline a comprehensive plan for promoting and supporting women in the business community within our mid-sized city.

656. My work for the city of New Orleans focuses on Income Inequality. Please help me explore strategies and policies to address income inequality and promote economic equity in our community.

657. I am the Future of Work Initiative Coordinator for the city of Tucson. Please help me describe a "Future of Work" initiative that prepares our community for technological changes, ensuring our workforce remains competitive and adaptable in the evolving job landscape.

658. I am a Recruiter for the city of Raleigh working on attracting remote workers to our city. Please help me outline strategies to attract remote workers to our community, leveraging their presence for economic growth.

659. I am the Immigrant Integration Coordinator for the city of San Antonio. Please help me outline a program aimed at integrating immigrants into the local economy and ensuring they contribute to our community's growth.

660. I am the Sustainability and Corporate Responsibility Manager for the city of Seattle. Please help me explore ways to incentivize corporate social responsibility within our business community.

661. I am the Affordable Healthcare Analyst for the city of Minneapolis. Please help me discuss the impact of affordable healthcare options on economic development and community well-being.

662. am the Community Engagement Manager for Economic Development in the city of Austin. Please help me outline methods to keep our citizens well-informed and actively involved in economic development initiatives.

663. How can the library better serve as a community hub?

664. How can libraries assist in bridging the digital divide in the community?

665. How can the library engage with community leaders to better serve the public?

666. Discuss how to create an inclusive strategic plan that addresses the needs of diverse community groups.

667. I am the Community Outreach Manager for the city of Nashville. Please help me plan how community outreach and citizen participation can be maintained over the long term.

668. I am the Director of Cultural Affairs for the city of New York. Please help me define the role of cultural institutions like museums, parks, and libraries in our city's strategic plan to enrich community life and encourage civic participation.

669. As a deputy city manager, how can I plan to use social media and other digital platforms to keep the community engaged and informed?

670. Community feedback is invaluable for assessing the effectiveness of implemented strategies and making necessary adjustments. Explain the mechanisms an assistant county

manager should plan to put in place for collecting and analyzing community feedback on the success of strategic initiatives. What specific mechanisms would you implement for gathering community feedback on the effectiveness of the city's or county's strategic initiatives?

671. A strategic plan is not a static document; it needs to be flexible and adaptable to changing community needs and external circumstances. Describe the system a city manager should establish for routinely revisiting and updating the strategic plan. How can we ensure that the strategic plan remains relevant and is adapted in line with evolving community needs and circumstances?

672. I am a Digital Communications Director for the City of ____. Digital platforms can enable better community engagement. Describe ways to use technology to boost community engagement. What digital platforms and strategies should I employ to enhance community engagement?

673. You are a Management Analyst in Parks and Recreation in the City of ____. Parks and recreation services contribute to community well-being. Describe your plans for parks and recreation. How will you improve the city's parks and recreation services?

674. I am the police chief for the city of ___. Describe a detailed plan to build and implement a community policing strategy.

675. As an Environmental Services Director for the City of ___, implement a plan to monitor and improve water quality that ensures the community has access to clean and safe water.

676. As a Building Inspector for the City of ___, I understand that regular building inspections are crucial for community safety. Discuss how I can ensure the effectiveness of building inspection and what methods I could explore and implement to make building inspections more effective and comprehensive?

677. I am a Senior Services Director for ____ County. Elderly

populations have specific needs that require specialized services. Please recommend plans for enhancing elderly care services and include initiatives to improve services for the elderly in the community?

678. I am a Historic Preservation Officer for ___ County. Please help me develop a plan for managing and promoting the preservation of historic landmarks and neighborhoods, thereby enriching our community heritage.

679. I am a city manager, and I am beginning the annual strategic planning process. Please help me create a step-by-step process for identifying the strategic goals for this year. Help me include all 7 of my departments (building services, community services police, fire, finance, HR, public works).

680. I am a Community Engagement Coordinator working in Oaksville. Please help me develop strategies to increase civic participation and community involvement among residents.

681. I am a Parks and Recreation Director working in Riverdale. Please help me plan and organize outdoor events and recreational activities to promote community bonding and well-being.

682. I am a Public Health Coordinator working in Lakeside. Please help me develop public health campaigns and programs to improve the overall well-being of our community.

683. I am a Housing Development Planner working in Pinecrest. Please help me devise strategies for affordable housing projects and community development plans.

684. In your role as the Transit Route Planner in Mobile, propose ways to optimize transit routes to better serve our community's needs while minimizing costs.

685. Assume the position of Transit Community Engagement Liaison in Florence. Share strategies for engaging with the local community to better align transit services with their needs and expectations.

686. In your role as the Paramedic Supervisor in Alexandria, propose ways to enhance the quality of emergency medical services provided to our community.

687. You're the Emergency Preparedness Coordinator in Arlington. Propose initiatives and policies to ensure our community is prepared for natural disasters and emergencies.

688. In your role as the Community Outreach Specialist in Savannah, describe strategies for engaging with local communities and promoting city initiatives.

689. Imagine you're the Community Events Coordinator in Albany. Share your strategy for organizing and promoting city-sponsored events to enhance community involvement.

GOVERNANCE & ADMINISTRATION

690. I am the city clerk in Fountain Hills, AZ I need to create a call to the public form for our city council meetings. Please create the form and make it comply with Arizona revised statutes.

691. You are a management analyst for the ____. the following is a chart of state shared revenues for cities and towns in arizona. I want you to pull out insights on Camp Verde.

692. Create a job description for an assistant to the city manager position for the city of Pasco WA; use language from here: https://www.pasco-wa.gov/832/City-Council-2022-2023-Goals.

693. I want to write a cover letter for a job based on two sources of info: [City Strategic Plan] and [Recruitment posting]. Address it to the mayor and council by name and sign it from [your name]

694. I want to compare these two OT reports. What can PD learn from FD and vice versa in OT management? As a city manager, what can I do to better manage OT costs?

695. I am a city clerk in cottonwood, az. Please help me create a public comment form for a council meeting. make it comply with ARS 38-431.

696. I am giving a presentation at a City Council meeting. Please summarize the following and help me put it into a presentation format.

697. I am the waste management manager for the city of___. How

can we reduce waste in public events and facilities?

698. I am the stormwater management supervisor for the city of ___. How can we improve stormwater management to prevent flooding?

699. What are the benefits of centralized versus decentralized fleet management?

700. How can we implement a life-cycle approach to asset management?

701. What are the benefits of using asset management software?

702. How can we integrate asset management with other municipal departments?

703. Suggest methods for effective grant management and reporting.

704. How can we improve the management of municipal debt?

705. In your role as the Asset Lifecycle Management Strategist in Willowbrook Meadows, describe a comprehensive plan for effective asset lifecycle management.

706. Describe the cost-benefit analysis for implementing a new financial management system.

707. How can we improve the process of vendor selection and contract management?

708. Describe techniques for stress management in the workplace.

709. I am working on managing a multi-generational workforce in Plano, Texas. What considerations should be kept in mind for effective management?

710. I am working on HR's role in crisis management in McKinney, Texas. How can HR contribute effectively to crisis management?

711. I am working on talent management solutions in Newark. What creative solutions can we implement to address talent

shortages in specific departments?

712. I am working on parking management for the city of Baltimore. Please help me explore ways to improve parking solutions in urban areas, such as implementing smart parking systems, optimizing on-street parking, and promoting alternative transportation options.

713. I am a Wildlife Management Specialist working on strategies for managing urban wildlife for the city of Decatur. Please help me explore methods like wildlife corridors, habitat preservation, and public education to coexist harmoniously with urban wildlife.

714. I am working on better utilizing water features in parks for both recreation and sustainability in Franklin. Please help me discuss options such as water-based recreational activities, stormwater management, and aquatic habitats that harness the potential of water features in our parks.

715. I am working on sustainable waste management in parks for the city of Hammond. Please help me describe a strategy that incorporates waste reduction, recycling stations, and eco-friendly disposal practices to minimize environmental impact.

716. I am working on measuring and tracking park usage for the city of Sterling Heights. Please help me outline methods for gathering data on park attendance, user demographics, and popular amenities to inform park management decisions.

717. In Davenport, we employ safe pest control methods in parks by using integrated pest management (IPM) strategies, which prioritize non-toxic solutions, wildlife-friendly practices, and monitoring to minimize environmental impact.

718. In Kearney, we maintain the quality of park water bodies through regular water quality testing, invasive species management, and ecological restoration efforts to preserve the natural beauty and health of our aquatic environments.

719. I am working on data-driven park management for the city

of North Little Rock's Parks and Recreation Department. Please help me explore how we can use data analytics to improve visitor experience, tailoring our services and amenities to meet their preferences and needs.

720. How can you use customer relationship management (CRM) software to improve library services?

721. How can you effectively engage the city council or county board in strategic planning?

722. I am the Internal Communications Manager for Adams County. Please help me strategize ways to improve communication between executive management and frontline staff.

723. Describe the steps for crisis management and contingency planning.

724. Describe how you would manage dissent or opposition to the strategic plan from council members or the public.

725. I am the City Council Liaison for the city of Detroit. Please help me develop a plan to keep the council or board updated on the progress of our strategic initiatives.

FIRE DEPARTMENT

726. I am the fire chief in Brentwood. Please tell me what steps I need to take and how I can support and enhance this 2030 plan for my city.

727. You are the City Manager of ____. Provide 3 actionable ways for the fire department to progress towards the four priorities in the City's strategic plan listed below. I want a 3-pronged actionable way for the department to contribute to each objective in the City's strategic plan.

728. i am the fire chief of brentwood tn. please summarize and give me insights on this strategic plan. make it relevant to the fire department.

729. Give me examples of how fire and EMS are using AI

730. you are a deputy city manager and oversee all of public safety. You are tasked with determining the capacity and current productivity levels of the fire department. create a plan to get and analyze the data that helps to determine capacity levels.

731. You are the City Manager of Fountain Hills, AZ. Provide 3 actionable ways for the fire department to progress towards the four priorities in the City's strategic plan listed below. I want a 3-pronged actionable way for the department to contribute to each objective in the City's strategic plan.

732. Please summarize the key duties and responsibilities of an Assistant Fire Chief.

733. I want to know the distinctions and overlap between Fire Marshal, CBO, and Fire Inspector duties.

734. Explain how it does and does not make sense to consolidate the duties of a fire marshal into the building official. Detail why some cities choose to do that while other cities have the roles seperated?

735. I am working on fire safety enhancements in residential areas in Hiliard. Can you suggest measures to enhance fire safety in our residential neighborhoods?

736. I am a Youth Education Coordinator working in Greenfield. Please help me explore initiatives to increase fire safety awareness among children.

737. Coordinated emergency responses are crucial for public safety. I am an Emergency Services Coordinator for the ___ Fire Department. Recommend strategies for improving emergency response coordination and improving the coordination of emergency services?

738. As the Fire Chief in Richmond, describe a strategy for improving emergency response times and coordination within the city.

739. Assume the position of Fire Prevention Specialist in Newport News. Outline a plan to educate the public about fire prevention and safety measures.

740. As the Firefighter Recruiter in Roanoke, describe how to attract and select qualified candidates to join our fire department.

741. Assume the position of Fire Safety Educator in Suffolk. Discuss methods for educating schools, businesses, and residents about fire safety and prevention.

PUBLIC WORKS

742. Make the following draft email to my Public Works Director nicer and more professional.

743. I am a public works director. I want to understand and help my team understand this strategic plan. Please summarize and give me bullets that help my team meet the strategic plan from the public works perspective.

744. The City of Whitewater Wisconsin Public Works Department is closing the northbound lane of South Whiton Street between West Peck Street and West Highland Street. The lane is expected to be closed from 9:00 AM to 4:00 PM from July 21 to July 25 for utility work. drivers should slow down and watch out for workers. Create a video advising such [use HeyGen plugin].

745. Please write a memo from the county manager to the county public works director that explains how public works can contribute to each objective in this strategic plan

746. I am the Public Works Director for the city of ___. Describe a feedback system to improve public services.

747. I am the public works director for the city___. How can we prioritize roads in need of immediate repair?

748. I am the public works director for the town of ___. Describe a program to improve the skills and qualifications of your team.

749. As a Regulatory Compliance Manager in Clearwater Falls, how would you design an internal audit system to ensure regulatory compliance within our public works department?

750. You're the Quality Assurance Supervisor in Willowbrook Springs. Share your insights on how we can revamp the quality assurance process for completed public works projects to deliver better results.

751. Assume the role of Performance Analyst in Redwood Cove. Define key performance indicators (KPIs) that would effectively measure the success of our public works projects.

752. As a Project Evaluation Specialist based in Silver Ridge, outline a step-by-step approach for conducting comprehensive post-project evaluations within our public works department.

753. As the Citizen Liaison Officer in Maplewood Hills, develop a streamlined process to address and resolve citizen complaints related to the quality of our public works projects.

DEVELOPMENT SERVICES

754. Create a job description for a Development Services Director ____.

755. Create a job description for a Development Services Director in ____. USE the following as a formatting template:

756. Create an RFP for the city of ____ for web development services. Use the following as template PROJECT OVERVIEW PROJECT SCOPE AND CURRENT SYSTEMS 6 3. PROJECT TIMELINE 7 4. VENDOR INSTRUCTIONS 8 5. VENDOR AND SYSTEM REQUIREMENTS 10 6. EVALUATION OF PROPOSALS 23 7. TERMS AND CONDITIONS

757. Create a job description for a Development Services Director in ____. USE the following as a formatting template: [Insert any job description with desired format]

758. I am the development services manager for the city of ___. How can we improve lighting in public spaces?

759. I am working on interdepartmental collaboration for the city of Frederick. Please help me discuss how development services can collaborate with other city departments for integrated planning, ensuring that land use, zoning, and infrastructure align effectively.

MEDIA RELATIONS

760. Create a press release for the hire of ____, Police Chief for the City ___. Highlight the following facts and accomplishments: _____.

761. How should the budget adapt to inflationary pressures?

762. You're the Press Secretary in Macon. Share your approach to managing media relations and ensuring accurate coverage of city events and policies.

POLICE DEPARTMENT

763. Develop a Sergeant's testing process for ___ Police Department

764. Based on this document (https://www.azcounties.org/DocumentCenter/View/3901/2023-Salary-and-Benefit-Survey-Combined-City-and-County) how competitive is the City of Apache Junction in hiring police officers?

765. Write a business case for the purchase of 25 Axon body 2 cameras for the ___ police department. Include a cost analysis.

766. I am the Human Resources director for the city of Burlington. I am requesting authorization from the city manager to prehire 2 additional police officers. this is because there are 2 police officers set to retire in September. and the police academy begins on December 12. please write a memo to the city manager, requesting such

767. I am a police chief for the city of bellingham wa. create a job description for a police LT, using the following as a template.

768. I am a police chief for the city of Bellingham WA, i need to create a job description for a police lieutenant. use the following as the template.

769. Explain why cities typically police and fire as separate departments have, while universities have police and fire under a public safety department

770. The following are the strategic objectives for the city of ___. I oversee the fire department, police department, police dispatch, code enforcement, and emergency management. Give me 5

actionable things my teams can do to make meaningful progress on each objective.

771. [upload public sector workforce data from the US Census Bureau] recommend 5 visualizations that allows me to compare police government function in the great lakes region

772. summarize this article and also tell me what parts might be relevant to police dispatch center

773. I need to study police dispatch center staffing models. Please give directions on how I can go about doing that.

PUBLIC SAFETY PLANNING

774. I want to walk my public safety leadership team through an internal threat assessment. Specifically, I want to discuss the question "What are the major internal threats facing your departments this year, in the next 2-5 years, and 5+ years" help craft the assessment matrix and a guide to the conversation.

775. I am working on inter-agency coordination for public safety in Columbus. How can we improve coordination and collaboration between different public safety agencies?

776. How can technology be leveraged to improve public safety in Cleveland?

777. I am working on enhancing security with local businesses in Cleveland. How can public safety agencies work more effectively with local businesses to enhance security?

778. I am working on safety planning for the city of Albany. How can we ensure the safety of vulnerable populations?

779. I am working on communication systems for public safety in Rochester. How can we improve our public safety communication systems to ensure more efficient responses?

780. I am working on ethics in public safety for the city of New York. What are some important ethical considerations we should take into account when developing public safety policies?

781. I am working on accountability measures for public safety

agencies in Syracuse. How can we increase transparency and accountability within our public safety agencies?

782. I am working on managing public safety during tourist seasons in Rochester. What challenges and solutions should we consider maintaining safety during peak tourist seasons?

783. I am working on resilience planning for public safety in Yonkers. How can we incorporate resilience planning into our public safety strategies to better respond to emergencies?

784. I am working on collaboration with educational institutions for public safety in Albany. How can public safety agencies collaborate more effectively with educational institutions to enhance safety?

785. I am a Social Media Coordinator working in Oaksville. Please help me explore how we can use social media to improve public safety communication.

786. I am an Event Safety Manager working in Riverdale. Please help me describe the considerations for public safety in large sporting events.

787. I am a Public Safety Coordinator working in Sunville. Please help me explore how public safety can be ensured during political rallies or protests.

788. I am an Animal Control Officer working in Pinecrest. Please help me explore how animal control can contribute to public safety.

789. I am a Public Safety Analyst working in Willowbrook. Please help me describe an approach for continuous improvement in public safety measures.

790. I am a Technology Integration Specialist working in Willowbrook. Please help me explore how we can manage public safety concerns associated with emerging technologies.

791. I am a Power Outage Preparedness Specialist working in Sunville. Please help me explore how we can maintain public

safety during extended power outages.

792. I am a Management Analyst working in Oaksville. Please help me discuss the challenges in ensuring public safety in rural versus urban areas.

793. I am a Data Analytics Specialist working in Oaksville. Please help me explore how we can improve data collection and analytics in public safety.

794. I am a Public Space Safety Planner working in Lakeside. Please help me explore the considerations for public safety in designing public spaces.

795. I am a Climate Change Resilience Specialist working in Meadowbrook. Please help me explore how public safety agencies can adapt to climate change challenges.

796. I am a Labor Dispute Preparedness Coordinator working in Harmonyville. Please help me suggest a strategy for maintaining public safety during strikes or labor disputes.

797. I am a Volunteer Engagement Specialist working in Willowbrook. Please help me explore how we can integrate volunteer organizations into public safety planning.

798. I am working on drone integration for Jefferson County, KY. Please help me explore how we can use drones to improve public safety.

799. I am working on the wellbeing of public safety personnel for Daviess County, KY. Please help me explore how we can ensure the wellbeing and work-life balance of public safety personnel.

800. I am working on public safety concerns unique to coastal or border areas for Horry County, SC. Please help me identify public safety concerns unique to coastal or border areas.

801. I am working on public art and safety for Weber County, UT. Please help me explore how public art and design can contribute to public safety.

802. I am working on public safety during holidays and festivals for Charleston County, SC. Please help me consider the public safety considerations during holidays and festivals.

803. I am working on integration of private security firms for Cache County, UT. Please help me explore how private security firms can be better integrated into public safety planning.

804. I am working on urban planning and public safety for Jefferson County, KY. Please help me discuss the role of urban planning in public safety.

805. I am working on complaint and feedback mechanisms for public safety for Weber County, UT. Please help me explore how we can improve the complaint and feedback mechanisms for public safety services.

806. I am the Economic Development Strategist for the city of Des Moines. Please help me discuss the relationship between public safety measures and their impact on economic development within our city.

807. You are an Animal Control Officer. Proper animal control and welfare services are necessary for both public safety and animal well-being. Share your plans for managing animal control and welfare. What are your strategies for balancing public safety with animal welfare?

SOFTWARE MANAGEMENT

808. You are a city fleet manager. You want to purchase software called TrackIT that enables GPS tracking of city fleet vehicles. Please draft a business case memo that outlines why this is a good investment by the city. The cost is 5,000 for the initial setup and about 500 per year for the entire fleet.

809. I am an IT Manager working on software license compliance for Philadelphia. Evaluate the feasibility of migrating to a cloud-based software solution for finance management.

810. I am a Project Coordinator working on migrating to a new project management tool for Pittsburgh. Research and propose three alternatives for the current project management software.

811. I am a Systems Analyst working on evaluating cloud-based solutions for the Finance Department of Allentown. Conduct a cost-benefit analysis for the top 3 cloud-based solutions.

812. I am an IT Specialist working on regular software updates and patches for Erie. Create a quarterly update schedule.

813. I am a Procurement Officer working on selecting a CRM system for Reading. Develop a checklist for evaluating CRM systems.

814. I am a Human Resources Officer working on implementing new HRIS software for Scranton. List the steps for successful implementation.

815. I am a Data Analyst working on assessing the effectiveness of our current data visualization software for Bethlehem. Evaluate its user-friendliness and scalability.

816. I am an IT Director working on a cybersecurity strategy for our software platforms in Lancaster. Outline a cybersecurity framework.

817. I am a Software Developer working on custom solutions for the Public Works Department of Harrisburg. Propose ideas for custom software features that could improve workflow.

818. I am a Network Administrator working on optimizing software for remote work for Altoona. Recommend security measures for remote access.

819. I am a Digital Transformation Lead working on phasing out legacy systems for York. Develop a timeline for the phase-out.

820. I am an IT Support Specialist working on staff training for new software features for State College. Create a training curriculum.

821. I am a Compliance Officer working on ensuring all software licenses are up to date for Wilkes-Barre. Develop a system for tracking and renewing software licenses.

822. I am a Security Analyst working on software vulnerability assessments for Easton. Conduct a vulnerability assessment and propose mitigations.

823. I am a Business Analyst working on a cost-benefit analysis of open-source office software for Lebanon. Prepare a report comparing open-source and proprietary office software.

824. I am a Training Coordinator working on a user manual for our new finance software for Williamsport. Write a draft for the user manual's introduction and table of contents.

825. I am a Quality Assurance Analyst working on software testing for upcoming releases for New Castle. Develop test cases for the new software features.

INFRASTRUCTURE & DEVELOPMENT

826. Please help me create the presentation on the importance of Investing in Infrastructure for Sustainable Growth for Cities and Communities

827. I am the IT Director for the city of ___. Describe how to update the municipality's IT infrastructure.

828. I am the streets manager for the city of ___. Describe a strategy to minimize traffic congestion during peak construction times.

829. Suggest ways to maintain infrastructure during extreme weather conditions.

830. Mentorship and apprenticeship programs can be invaluable for skill development. Can you outline an effective program that facilitates knowledge transfer and professional growth among our team members?

831. In your role as Infrastructure Durability Manager in Pineview Heights, propose strategies and methods to ensure the long-term durability of our public infrastructure projects.

832. I am working on Transportation Infrastructure for Yavapai County, AZ. Please help me suggest methods for improving transportation infrastructure in Yavapai County, such as expanding road networks, enhancing public transit, and promoting sustainable transportation options.

833. I am working on Smart City Initiatives for Kenosha County, WI. Please help me outline methods for implementing smart city technologies in Kenosha County, considering data-driven solutions, IoT integration, and digital infrastructure.

834. I am working on Waste Management for Yuma County, AZ. Please help me describe how we can improve waste management practices in new developments in Yuma County, emphasizing recycling, sustainable waste disposal, and waste reduction.

835. I am working on Disaster-Resistant Construction for Cochise County, AZ. Please help me outline best practices for disaster-resistant construction in Cochise County, considering resilience against natural disasters and climate change.

836. I am working on transportation infrastructure for Orange County. Please help me suggest methods for improving transportation infrastructure in Orange County, such as expanding road networks, enhancing public transit, and promoting sustainable transportation options.

837. I am working on smart city initiatives for King County. Please help me outline methods for implementing smart city technologies in King County, considering data-driven solutions, IoT integration, and digital infrastructure.

838. I am working on waste management for Multnomah County. Please help me describe how we can improve waste management practices in new developments in Multnomah County, emphasizing recycling, sustainable waste disposal, and waste reduction.

839. I am working on disaster-resistant construction for Miami-Dade County. Please help me outline best practices for disaster-resistant construction in Miami-Dade County, considering resilience against natural disasters and climate change.

840. I am working on tourism development for the city of Annapolis. Please help me describe a strategy for boosting local tourism through development, which may involve creating

tourism-friendly infrastructure, promoting cultural attractions, and enhancing the visitor experience.

841. I am working on ethical development practices for the city of Bowie. Please help me explore how we can ensure ethical practices in property development, including transparency measures, ethical guidelines, and public accountability.

842. I am working on architectural innovation for the city of Laurel. Please help me outline ways to foster innovation in architectural design, embracing cutting-edge technology, sustainable principles, and creative approaches to urban development.

843. I am working on construction waste management for the city of Cumberland. Please help me identify best practices for construction waste management, including recycling initiatives, waste reduction measures, and responsible disposal methods.

844. I am a Transportation Planner working on improving accessibility to public transport stations in Mitchell. Please help me describe methods such as accessible pathways, transit-oriented development, and digital information systems that enhance public transport access for all residents.

845. I am an Environmental Planner working on strategies for increasing green spaces and urban forests in Huron. Please help me identify opportunities for urban tree planting, park expansion, and green infrastructure projects to enhance our city's greenery.

846. I am a Development Analyst working on improving the development permit review process for the city of Aurora. Please help me describe methods such as streamlining procedures, offering digital application options, and enhancing communication with applicants to expedite the permit review process.

847. I am a Data Analyst working on transparent reporting on development metrics for the city of Rockford. Please help

me outline strategies for collecting and sharing data related to development projects, including key performance indicators and progress reports accessible to the public.

848. I am an Environmental Planner working on implementing water-saving features in new developments for the city of Joliet. Please help me discuss methods like rainwater harvesting, low-flow fixtures, and drought-resistant landscaping to promote water conservation in new construction.

849. I am an Environmental Sustainability Specialist working on incorporating modern waste sorting and recycling facilities in new developments for the city of Arlington Heights. Please help me discuss strategies for designing sustainable waste management systems, recycling centers, and waste-to-energy initiatives that align with environmental goals.

850. I am a Sustainability Analyst working on incentivizing sustainable building practices for the city of Chandler. Please help me explore strategies such as green building incentives, renewable energy integration, and sustainable materials to promote eco-friendly construction.

851. I am an Urban Planner working on improving transit-oriented development for the city of Tempe. Please help me outline ways to enhance public transportation, pedestrian access, and mixed-use development around transit hubs to create sustainable and accessible communities.

852. I am an Environmental Planner working on reducing the carbon footprint of new developments for the city of Buckeye. Please help me identify sustainable construction practices, renewable energy integration, and green transportation options to minimize carbon emissions.

853. I am a Stormwater Management Specialist working on handling stormwater management in urban areas for the city of Casa Grande. Please help me describe techniques such as permeable pavement, retention ponds, and stormwater

infrastructure to mitigate urban flooding and water pollution.

854. I am working on sports facilities and infrastructure improvement for the city of Detroit. Please help me explore how we can enhance our sports facilities by upgrading fields, courts, and lighting, and by creating multi-sport complexes to accommodate various recreational activities.

855. I am working on green space development for the city of Little Rock's Parks and Recreation Department. Please help me describe a plan for a rooftop garden or park, maximizing greenery and recreational opportunities in urban settings.

856. I am the Inclusive Play Area Development Specialist for the city of Seattle. Please help me explore strategies for creating inclusive play areas that children of all abilities can enjoy, promoting accessibility and inclusivity in our parks.

857. I am the Commercial Space Redevelopment Specialist for the city of Anchorage. Please help me suggest methods for redeveloping unused commercial spaces, revitalizing our urban areas.

858. I am the Workforce Development Strategist for the city of Burlington. Please help me describe our strategy for workforce development, ensuring our residents have the skills needed for the jobs of the future.

859. I am the Infrastructure Optimization Manager for the city of Helena. Please help me explore how infrastructure can be optimized to facilitate economic growth, from transportation to utilities.

860. I am the E-commerce Development Advisor for the city of Boise. Please help me explore how local government can facilitate the growth of e-commerce businesses within our city.

861. I am the Agriculture and Rural Development Coordinator for the city of Helena. Please help me identify ways our city can support agriculture and rural development to enhance our local

economy.

862. I am the Technology and Innovation Hub Development Manager for the city of Concord. Please help me discuss strategies for developing technology and innovation hubs that can drive economic growth and innovation.

863. I am the Air and Sea Connectivity Enhancement Director for the city of Tulsa. Please help me identify methods to improve air and sea connectivity, enhancing transportation infrastructure for economic growth.

864. I am the Development Director for the city of Baton Rouge. Please help me devise a plan to establish a reputation as a "green city" and explore the economic implications and benefits associated with sustainability initiatives in our mid-sized city.

865. I am the Tourism Development Manager for the city of Louisville. Please help me outline a plan for our mid-sized city to become a center for medical tourism, attracting visitors from near and far.

866. I am the Workforce Development Director for the city of Los Angeles. Please help me outline strategies to reduce unemployment and enhance job opportunities for our residents.

867. I am the Technology Infrastructure Manager for the city of Miami. Please help me describe a comprehensive plan for implementing a city-wide WiFi network to enhance connectivity for our residents and businesses.

868. I am the Construction and Renovation Advisor for the city of Phoenix. Please help me outline some effective ways to support the home renovation and construction industries in our city.

869. How can libraries contribute to workforce development?

870. I am the Housing and Urban Development Director for the city of Tucson. Please help me address how our strategic plan can solve issues related to affordable housing and urban development.

871. I am the Leadership Development Consultant for the city

of Charlotte. Please help me outline how we can prepare for leadership transitions without disrupting our strategic objectives.

872. I am an urban planner for the city of ___. Please help me develop a plan for improving biking and pedestrian infrastructure that helps make the city more walkable and bike friendly.

PUBLIC SAFETY

873. You are Road EngineerGPT for the city of ____. Recommend ways to improve the safety of pedestrian crossings?

874. I am a traffic engineer for the city of ___. Describe a plan to improve pedestrian safety in high-traffic areas.

875. I am the public works manager for the city of __. How can we ensure the safety of construction zones?

876. Assume the position of Essential Services Preservation Planner in Elmwood Glen. Outline essential services that must be maintained during any financial emergency and how to do so.

877. Suggest security measures for protecting financial data.

878. I am working on enhancing workplace safety in Muskogee, Oklahoma. What safety measures and initiatives can we implement to create a safer work environment?

879. I am working on optimizing emergency response times in Toledo. What measures and strategies can we implement to improve emergency response times?

880. I am working on improving traffic safety in Cleveland. What suggestions do you have for enhancing traffic safety in our city?

881. I am working on improving school safety in Akron. Can you describe a comprehensive plan for enhancing school safety?

882. I am working on improving public transportation safety in Albany. What suggestions do you have for making our public transportation system safer?

883. I am working on handling mental health crisis incidents

for Buffalo. What strategies can we implement to better handle incidents involving mental health crises and ensure safety?

884. I am a Pedestrian Safety Specialist working in Lakeside. Please help me describe methods for improving the safety of pedestrian areas.

885. I am a Water Safety Coordinator working in Meadowbrook. Please help me identify methods for improving water safety.

886. I am an Emergency Planning Coordinator working in Meadowbrook. Please help me identify guidelines for emergency evacuation planning.

887. I am a Food Safety Coordinator working in Pinecrest. Please help me describe methods for ensuring food safety during large public events.

888. I am an Emergency Planning and Review Officer working in Hillside. Please help me describe a process for regular review and update of emergency plans.

889. I am a Workplace Safety Consultant working in Sunville. Please help me suggest measures for reducing workplace accidents.

890. I am a Safety Inspector working on ways to ensure safety in public construction projects in Yankton. Please help me outline safety protocols, contractor guidelines, and quality control measures to maintain a safe environment during construction.

891. I am working on maintaining the safety of park visitors for the city of Evansville. Please help me identify methods including regular safety inspections, effective lighting, and clear signage to ensure the well-being of park-goers.

892. I am working on ensuring that parks remain safe and welcoming after dark in Anderson. Please help me outline strategies such as well-lit pathways, nighttime events, and security patrols to maintain a secure environment for evening park visitors.

893. I am working on improving walking and cycling paths for the city of Ann Arbor. Please help me describe a plan to enhance our walking and cycling paths, focusing on connectivity, safety, and accessibility for pedestrians and cyclists.

894. I am working on pet-friendly areas integration for the city of Lansing's parks. Please help me explore how we can effectively integrate pet-friendly areas within our parks, providing designated spaces for dogs and their owners while ensuring cleanliness and safety.

895. In North Platte, we keep parking equipment well-maintained and up to date through regular inspections, repairs, and replacement cycles, ensuring the safety and enjoyment of park users.

896. In South Sioux City, we make parks more appealing and safer for solo visitors through increased lighting, improved wayfinding signage, and regular patrols by park rangers to enhance security and comfort.

897. I am working on safety and emergency planning for the city of Rogers' Parks and Recreation Department. Please help me identify ways to develop effective evacuation and first-aid strategies in our parks, ensuring the well-being of visitors.

898. I am working on facility management for the city of Hot Springs' Parks and Recreation Department. Please help me identify ways to ensure that park facilities meet health and safety standards, providing a secure and enjoyable environment for all.

899. I am the Creative Lighting Solutions Planner for the city of FT Lauderdale. Please help me discuss how we can implement creative lighting solutions that are both functional and beautiful in our parks, enhancing their ambiance and safety.

900. I am the Security Manager for the library system in Hancock County. Please help me outline what steps can be taken to improve security across our libraries.

901. You are a Transportation Advisor for ___ RTA. The efficiency and safety of public transportation are key concerns for local government. Discuss potential upgrades to public transportation systems. What are some key upgrades you would suggest for improving public transportation?

902. I am a Traffic Safety Officer working in Meadowbrook. Please help me enhance road safety through effective traffic management, public awareness campaigns, and infrastructure improvements.

903. In your role as the Medical Director of the Emergency Department in Virginia Beach, discuss strategies for improving patient care and outcomes.

904. Imagine you're the EMS Quality Assurance Analyst in Hampton. Share how you would monitor and improve the quality of emergency medical services provided by our department.

905. Assume the position of Safety Coordinator in High Point. Discuss how you would develop and implement safety programs to reduce workplace accidents and incidents.

906. In your capacity as the Emergency Preparedness Specialist in Winston-Salem, outline a comprehensive plan for emergency response and disaster preparedness within the city.

907. As the Loss Control Consultant in Fayetteville, share your methods for advising city departments on loss prevention strategies and safety measures.

PUBLIC RELATIONS

908. I am the PIO for ___ Sheriffs Department. How can we better handle public relations during a crisis?

909. I am the Public Relations Manager for the city of Chicago. Please help me plan how to manage public expectations during the implementation of our strategic plan to maintain trust and facilitate communication.

910. As the Public Relations Specialist in Sandy Springs, outline a plan for improving the city's public image and reputation.

COMMUNITY
SERVICES

911. I am a parks and rec director, for the city of ___. Suggest enhancements to recreational facilities.

912. I am the utilities services manager for the city of ___. Propose an initiative for water conservation awareness among residents.

913. I am a parks and recreation manager for the city of ___. Suggest ways to make playgrounds and parks safer.

914. What are some immediate cost-cutting measures that can be implemented without affecting public services?

915. I am working on incorporating eco-friendly designs into recreational facilities in Clarksville. Please help me identify methods like sustainable materials, energy-efficient lighting, and rainwater harvesting that can minimize the environmental footprint of our facilities.

916. I am working on making parks more accessible to people with disabilities in Lafayette. Please help me suggest methods such as accessible pathways, inclusive play structures, and sensory gardens to ensure that our parks are welcoming and usable for all residents.

917. I am working on a strategy for natural habitat preservation within park systems for the city of Jackson. Please help me discuss conservation efforts, wildlife corridors, and habitat restoration initiatives that protect and enhance our natural environments.

918. I am working on using technology to improve the park visitor experience in Clarksville. Please help me describe the implementation of mobile apps, interactive maps, augmented reality, and Wi-Fi access to enhance the digital aspect of our parks.

919. I am working on child-friendly park designs for the city of Indianapolis. Please help me explore key considerations such as safe playground equipment, age-appropriate activities, accessible amenities, and shaded areas to create enjoyable and secure environments for children.

920. I am working on designing parks to serve multiple generations in Fort Wayne. Please help me outline how we can incorporate features like multi-use trails, fitness stations, and gathering spaces to cater to the recreational needs of people of all ages, from children to seniors.

921. I am working on making seasonal adaptations to parks and recreational facilities in Carmel. Please help me discuss how we can modify facilities and activities to accommodate changing seasons, from winter ice rinks to summer concert series.

922. I am working on introducing unique recreational activities to attract more visitors to Gary's parks. Please help me brainstorm distinctive activities like disc golf courses, outdoor fitness challenges, or astronomy nights that can draw new interest and participation.

923. I am working on optimizing traffic and parking near popular recreational areas in Terre Haute. Please help me discuss solutions such as efficient parking layouts, shuttle services, and bike-sharing programs to manage congestion and enhance accessibility.

924. I am working on including public art in parks for the city of Muncie. Please help me explore ways to integrate sculptures, murals, and installations that enhance the artistic and cultural appeal of our parks, making them more engaging and enriching spaces for visitors.

925. I am working on how parks can contribute to local tourism for the city of Traverse City. Please help me discuss how parks can be positioned as tourist attractions, emphasizing their natural beauty, recreational opportunities, and cultural events to draw visitors to our city.

926. I am working on integrating smart technologies into our parks, such as Wi-Fi and charging stations, for the city of Warren. Please help me describe how we can incorporate these technologies without disrupting the natural beauty of our parks, ensuring they enhance the visitor experience.

927. In Iowa City, we improve signage and information available in parks by updating signage to be more informative and user-friendly, creating digital maps and apps for park navigation, and involving local artists in designing educational signs.

928. In Ames, we involve schools in educational programs focused on nature and conservation by developing curriculum-aligned outdoor education programs, organizing field trips to parks, and collaborating with teachers to incorporate nature-based learning into their lessons.

929. In Dubuque, we maintain historical landmarks within parks by conducting regular inspections, performing necessary repairs and renovations, and partnering with local historical preservation organizations to ensure these landmarks are well-preserved and accessible to the public.

930. In Milwaukee, we make parks more attractive destinations during winter months by organizing seasonal events like ice skating rinks, winter festivals, and cross-country skiing trails, offering a variety of cold-weather activities for residents to enjoy.

931. In Green Bay, we integrate local history into park designs by creating historical markers, installing interpretive signage, and collaborating with local historians and museums to tell the stories of our city's past within the park environment.

932. In Appleton, we provide adequate restroom facilities without

compromising park aesthetics by designing restroom buildings that blend harmoniously with the park environment, utilizing natural materials and landscaping for an attractive appearance.

933. In Waukesha, we reduce noise pollution in parks near busy streets by installing sound barriers, utilizing landscaping for noise absorption, and implementing quiet hours to minimize disturbances during specific times.

934. In Eau Claire, we enhance the botanical variety within parks by establishing native plant gardens, wildflower meadows, and butterfly-friendly habitats, fostering biodiversity and creating attractive natural spaces.

935. In Janesville, we accommodate varying levels of physical ability in outdoor activities and trails by incorporating accessible pathways, adaptive equipment, and sensory-rich experiences to ensure everyone can enjoy our parks.

936. In the city of Omaha, we are working on promoting respectful behavior among park-goers by employing park rangers and implementing educational campaigns that encourage courteous and responsible use of our parks.

937. In Lincoln, we effectively communicate park rules and guidelines by using clear signage, distributing informational brochures, and utilizing digital channels like our city website and social media to keep park users informed.

938. In Hastings, we engage teenagers in park activities and programs by offering youth-focused events, sports leagues, and volunteer opportunities, providing recreational options that appeal to this demographic.

939. In Columbus, we create quiet zones for relaxation and meditation within parks by designating serene areas, adding seating, and promoting mindfulness and wellness activities.

940. In Scottsbluff, we offer concessions that are both profitable and healthy by partnering with local vendors to provide a variety

of nutritious food options and promoting healthy eating habits among park-goers.

941. In Beatrice, we integrate fitness equipment and exercise areas within parks to encourage physical activity and healthy lifestyles among residents, with options for individuals of all fitness levels.

942. In Alliance, we involve local artists in creating a dynamic park atmosphere by commissioning public art installations, hosting art festivals, and providing opportunities for artists to contribute to park aesthetics and culture.

943. I am working on landscape enhancement for the city of Fayetteville's Parks and Recreation Department. Please help me explore ways to maximize scenic viewpoints in our parks, offering breathtaking vistas for visitors to enjoy.

944. I am working on sustainability initiatives for the city of Springdale's Parks and Recreation Department. Please help me discuss how we can incorporate renewable energy solutions like solar panels in park designs, aligning with our commitment to environmental stewardship.

945. I am working on seasonal recreation planning for the city of Conway's Parks and Recreation Department. Please help me explore how we can better accommodate seasonal outdoor activities like sledding or fishing in our parks, providing diverse recreational options.

946. I am the Indoor Recreational Space Optimization Manager for the city of Portland. Please help me explore strategies for maximizing the usability of indoor recreational spaces, ensuring they cater to diverse needs and interests.

947. I am working on water conservation for the city of Flagstaff Parks and Recreation Department. Please help me describe methods for promoting water conservation within parks, aligning with sustainable practices and environmental stewardship.

948. I am working on Shelter and Seating Design for the city of Bend. Parks and Recreation Department. Please help me discuss ways to provide shelter and seating that seamlessly blend into park design, enhancing the overall aesthetics and comfort.

949. I am the Park Connectivity Planner for the city of Bozeman. Please help me explore how we can improve connectivity between different parks and recreational areas, creating a more integrated and accessible network for our residents.

950. I am a Park Ranger for the city of Maricopa Please help me explore ways to better handle lost and found items in a secure and organized manner within our parks, ensuring a smooth process for both staff and visitorsI am the Park Inspection and Quality Assurance Manager for the city of Portland. Please help me describe methods for regular park inspection and quality checks to ensure our parks remain safe and well-maintained.

951. I am the Educational Trails and Interpretive Signage Specialist for the city of Denver. Please help me describe how we can create educational trails that inform visitors about local flora and fauna, promoting environmental education in our parks.

952. I am the Local Products and Services Promotion Coordinator for the city of Santa Fe. Please help me identify ways to promote local products and services, supporting our homegrown businesses and artisans.

953. What strategies can be employed to encourage more frequent library visits?

954. Discuss ways to make the library more accessible to people with disabilities.

955. How can the library collaborate with local schools?

956. Describe a plan for a mobile library to serve rural or underserved areas.

957. What steps can be taken to modernize the library's computer systems?

958. Describe a campaign to encourage library membership.

959. Discuss ways the library can support local artists and creators.

960. What are some methods to better utilize library spaces for public events?

961. I am the Renewable Energy Manager for the library system in Davis County. Please help me describe a plan for implementing renewable energy solutions in our library buildings.

962. I am the Senior Services Coordinator for the library system in Douglas County. Please help me discuss ways the library can better serve the needs of our elderly population.

963. I am the Archivist for the library system in Clayton County. Please help me discuss methods for preserving historical documents and local archives in our library system.

964. I am the Social Media Coordinator for the library system in Fox County. Please help me strategize how to improve our library's social media presence.

965. How can the library assist in language learning and ESL programs?

966. How can the library support small businesses and entrepreneurs?

967. What are some innovative methods for cataloging library materials?

968. Describe a plan for an after-school program hosted at the library.

969. How can you use data analytics to improve library services?

970. Discuss ways to create a more sustainable and eco-friendlier library.

971. What are some methods for increasing volunteer participation at the library?

972. Describe a "maker space" and how it could be implemented in the library.

973. How can you improve in-library amenities, such as seating areas or study rooms?

974. What are some unique merchandise or retail opportunities for the library?

975. Discuss the ethical considerations of data collection in the library.

976. Describe a plan for hosting a library-based film or lecture series.

977. What methods can be used to manage and reduce library late fees?

978. Discuss the importance of interlibrary loans and how to optimize this service.

979. I am the Public Health Director in ____ County. Discuss how I can enhance mental health services. What are examples for expanding and improving mental health services?

980. As a Library Services Director, what initiatives could enhance and enrich library services?

981. I am a Senior Services Manager working in Hillside. Please help me develop programs and services to improve the quality of life for our senior residents, including healthcare access and social activities.

982. Imagine you're the Transit Technology Integration Manager in Dothan. Discuss how to integrate modern technologies to enhance the efficiency and convenience of our transit services.

LEGAL & COMPLIANCE

983. Effective record-keeping is indispensable for compliance. What innovative methods and tools can we employ to significantly enhance our record-keeping processes and ensure full compliance with all requirements?

984. In your role as the Payroll Audit Planner in Clearwater Harbor, describe a strategy for conducting periodic payroll audits to ensure accuracy and compliance.

985. What are the legal considerations in municipal contracting?

986. I am working on measures for promoting ethical conduct and compliance in Lake Worth, Florida. What measures can we implement for this purpose?

987. I am an Accessibility Coordinator working on ensuring accessibility in public spaces for the city of Yuma. Please help me explore strategies like ADA compliance, universal design, and accessible transportation options to enhance accessibility for all residents.

DIGITAL TRANSFORMATION

988. I am working on best practices for digital and paper record-keeping in Melbourne, Florida. What are these best practices?

989. My work focuses on Digital Transformation for the city of Fresno. Please help me outline strategies to support local businesses in adopting digital transformation, enhancing their competitiveness and growth.

990. I am the Broadband Expansion Strategist for the city of Tucson. Please help me discuss how broadband internet access can be expanded to benefit our local economy and increase digital inclusion.

991. I am the Chief Information Officer for the city of San Francisco. Please help me describe a framework for digital transformation that aligns with the city's strategic goals.

PLANNING AND ZONING

992. I am working on Accessibility Planning for Rutherford County, TN. Please help me explore how we can ensure that new developments in Rutherford County are accessible to people with disabilities, focusing on inclusive design and compliance with accessibility standards.

993. I am working on Land Use Planning for Mohave County, AZ. Please help me discuss how we can optimize land use in Mohave County, considering factors like zoning, mixed-use developments, and sustainable land management.

994. I am working on Urban Planning for Madison County, TN. Please help me explore strategies for reducing urban sprawl in Madison County, focusing on compact development, efficient land use, and smart growth principles.

995. I am working on accessibility planning for Fairfax County. Please help me explore how we can ensure that new developments in Fairfax County are accessible to people with disabilities, focusing on inclusive design and compliance with accessibility standards.

996. I am working on land use planning for San Diego County. Please help me discuss how we can optimize land use in San Diego County, considering factors like zoning, mixed-use developments, and sustainable land management.

997. I am working on urban planning for Travis County. Please

help me explore strategies for reducing urban sprawl in Travis County, focusing on compact development, efficient land use, and smart growth principles.

998. I am working on sustainability planning for the city of Rockville. Please help me outline strategies for incorporating renewable energy sources into new developments, including solar panel installations, green building standards, and sustainable infrastructure design.

999. I am working on adaptive reuse planning for the city of College Park. Please help me discuss strategies for the adaptive reuse of old buildings, including incentives for preservation, innovative redevelopment ideas, and recognizing historical significance.

1000. I am an Infrastructure Planner working on promoting the use of electric cars through infrastructure development for the city of Brookings. Please help me discuss the installation of charging stations, incentives for electric vehicle adoption, and sustainable transportation planning.

1001. I am a Climate Resilience Coordinator working on integrating climate change resilience into development planning for the city of Pierre. Please help me discuss strategies like flood mitigation, green infrastructure, and disaster preparedness measures to address climate-related challenges.